Doll Artists at Work

VOLUME ONE

BY *Kathleen Ryan*

Featuring 25 of today's top doll artists!

Kathy Barry-Hippensteel
Floyd Bell
Karen Blandford
Marilyn Bolden
Uta Brauser
Paul Crees & Peter Coe
Julie Good-Kruger
Hildegard Gunzel
Maggie Iacono
Wendy Lawton
Jerri McCloud
Cindy McClure
Jan McLean
Janet Ness
Betty "Wee" Paulson
Patricia Rose
Julia Rueger
Rotraut Schrott
Pat Secrist
FayZah Spanos
Sherry Stephens
Ruth Treffeisen
Susan Wakeen
Nancy Walters
G. F. "Fritz" Wolff

i

This publication is sold with the understanding that neither the publisher nor the author are engaged in rendering accounting, legal or other professional service. It is intended to provide correct information with regard to the subject matter covered. If legal or other expert advice is desired, the services of a competent professional person should be sought.

Some responses may have been edited for readability and flow.

Doll Artists at Work

Printed in the United States of America

ISBN 1-888076-01-1

Publisher: Infodial 13730 S.R. 84, Box 211, Davie, FL 33325
For information on bulk purchases and quantity discounts call 305-423-0820

Cover photo: Fritz Wolff and Gretchen Wolff of the Wimbledon Collection

TABLE OF CONTENTS

Acknowledgments

A special thanks to Patricia Blasi and Gloria Centi, of *P.G.'s Enchanted Dolls,* in Fort Lauderdale, Florida, for introducing me to the doll world and offering me a wealth of information.

Thanks to all 25 doll artists featured in this book for sharing so much of themselves with us, and for supplying the pictures used throughout this book.

Introduction

Today's fascination with art dolls goes beyond the beauty of the individual sculptures to a heightened interest in the talented creators behind them. As we learn about these gifted artists, we naturally feel closer to our dolls and develop a greater appreciation for the art itself.

Doll Artists At Work offers the reader unique insights into the creative process of 25 of today's top doll artists as they answer the questions most of us wonder about. How did they get started? What motivates them? Where do they get their ideas? How do they juggle dollmaking and family life? What techniques work best? How do they keep that creative edge? What was their worst disaster or greatest discovery?

The surprisingly candid and often humorous answers to these questions not only entertain the reader, but provide valuable and useful tips for both aspiring and established doll artists. Find out how these artists made it to the top. Learn many of their professional techniques, thoughts and secrets as they open their hearts and studios to us. Whether you are an adoring fan, an avid doll collector, or a doll artist yourself, you are sure to enjoy the personal and professional insights offered in this revealing book.

Chapter One

MEET THE DOLL ARTISTS

This book features 25 of today's most popular, highly successful doll artists. Their work represents dolls crafted from nearly every conceivable medium - earthenware, cloth, felt, porcelain, polymer clays, cellulose clays, wax-over-porcelain, poured wax, paper mache, resin, vinyl and wood - with prices ranging from a low of $50 to a high of over $10,000. To help familiarize you with these talented artists, we have included personal photographs and short biographies which briefly sketch out the highlights of each artist's background, the type of dolls they produce and the mediums they prefer to work in. For easy referencing, these biographies are presented in alphabetical order. Now, meet the artists.

Kathy Barry-Hippensteel of Des Plaines, IL, best known for her 12 to 15 inch chubby-cheeked toddlers created for *Ashton Drake*, has sculpted over 60 original concept dolls with themes of exploration from a typical day in a toddler's life. Each doll is produced in porcelain. In 1993, her *Tickles* was the number one top selling direct market doll in America.

Floyd Bell is a woodshop teacher at Westchester High School in Los Angeles, California, where the school founded the *Floyd Bell Gallery* in his honor. Though known best for his one-of-a-kind ethnic and historical dolls carved in wood, he has ventured into porcelain and bronze as well. In 1993 Bell founded *The Floyd Bell Scholarship Fund* to raise money for talented art students.

Karen Blandford of *Artist Originals by Karen*, in Pickton Australia, is known for her big-eyed, sultry beauties. Preferring to sculpt little girls and young ladies, Blandford produces elaborately costumed porcelain dolls in small limited editions. The dolls range in size from 24 - 36 inches.

Marilyn Bolden of *MARI-DAWN Dolls*, Clearwater, FL, began in 1986 as a portrait artist. Today she is best known for her heartwarming little girls and high fashion model dolls. With a degree in fashion design, Bolden produces limited edition and one-of-a-kind porcelain dolls ranging in size from 18 to 38 inches.

Uta Brauser, the German artist behind *Uta Brauser Designs, Inc.*, introduced her sculptures to America in 1988. They include one-of-a-kind period dolls and marionettes. She also created a line of highly successful contemporary *Black City Kids* for *Dynasty Dolls*. Her newest project is a multi-ethnic line of 13 inch children called *Amerikkan Kids*. The artist now lives in New York City.

Paul Crees and *Peter Coe* of the *Paul Crees Collection*, Dorset England, specialize in 20 to 28 inch limited edition poured-wax portrait dolls, inspired by some of the world's most beautiful women. Crees and Coe work together on all projects, calling on their extensive training in art, theater, and costume design. In March of 1994, in recognition of their artistic contribution, the artists received a *Jumeau Award* for their entire body of work.

Julie Good-Kruger, of *Good-Kruger Dolls* in Lancaster, PA, designs and produces limited edition children and baby dolls in porcelain and vinyl. The porcelain pieces are all porcelain with jointed bodies and are strung for movement. The vinyls are totally vinyl stand up children with jointed bodies. The artist also designs smaller dolls for *Ashton-Drake Galleries*.

Hildegard Gunzel has been sculpting fine porcelain and wax-over-porcelain dolls for over twenty years. Recipient of countless awards, her pieces stand in museums all over the world. The German based sculptress is also a renowned author in the doll making industry and one of the industries most sought after porcelain sculpting teachers.

5

Maggie Iacono, whose work is distributed solely through *European Artist Dolls* in Richmond Virginia, specializes in 18 inch fully sculpted felt dolls. Known for their perfectly smooth faces and innocent expressions, her one-of-a-kind and limited edition ball-jointed children reflect the essence of childhood. Iacono carefully chooses colors to enhance the mood of the piece, hand dying fabrics for just the right hue.

Wendy Lawton, of *Lawton Doll Company*, in Turlock, CA, has been making dolls since the late 1970s. A former teacher with a love of story telling, she is best known for her all porcelain storybook characters. In 1986 she formed a partnership with Linda Smith. The artist also designs for the *Ashton Drake Galleries*. In 1994 she introduced an innovative line of poseable dolls with fully jointed wooden bodies.

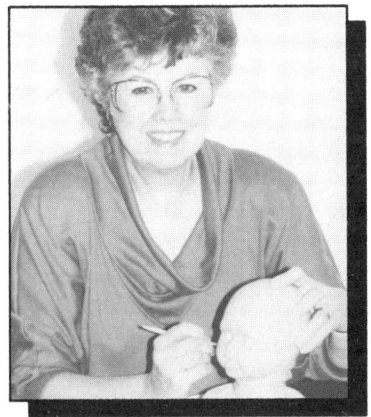

Jerri McCloud is the sculptress behind *Dolls by Jerri* of Charlotte, North Carolina. She and her husband, Jim, are referred to as the "grandparents" of the porcelain dollmaking industry, because they established the first commercial porcelain doll manufacturing company in the United States in 1976. Today the company produces fifty new dolls each year in porcelain and vinyl limited editions.

Cindy McClure of *Cindy McClure Originals*, began making fairies in 1984. Since then she has created limited edition and one-of-a-kind babies, little girls, boys, women, angels, and clowns in porcelain and wax over porcelain. The dolls range in size from 3 to 40 inches. McClure designs for *Victoria's Collectibles, Ashton Drake Galleries, QVC* and *HomeShopping.*

7

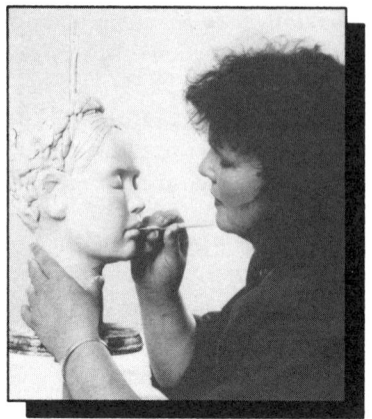

Jan McLean, artist for *Jan McLean Originals*, Dunegin, New Zealand, produces hand crafted porcelain dolls with an attitude. The young women dolls range in height from 32 to 50 inches, and are issued in small editions of 20 to 50 pieces. McLean is largely responsible for bringing the doll world to New Zealand by organizing doll conventions and launching an agressive publicity campaign.

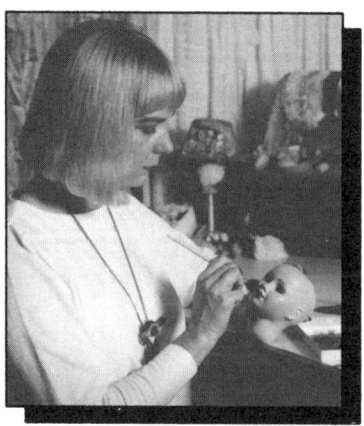

Janet Ness, of *J. NESS, designs* of Parker, Colorado, is best known for her 24 inch limited edition lines of beautiful young lady dolls sculpted in fine porcelain. This award-winning artist carried a degree in paleontology into the graphics design business, which surprisingly evolved into dollmaking.

Betty "Wee" Paulson, of Las Vegas, Nevada, creator of the soft sculpted *"Weedidits"* and past president of *NIADA (National Institute of American Doll Artists)*, has created over 1,700 one-of-a-kind pieces in felt during her 35 years of dollmaking. Most of her charming vignettes depict children in innocent exploration or rambunctious play. Her heartwarming scenes were reproduced by the *American Greetings Card Company* in dozens of highly successful series of cards.

Patricia Rose, of the *Patricia Rose Studio* in Anna Maria Florida, was a portrait artist before turning to dolls in 1989. Known for her one-of-a-kind and limited edition porcelain children with innocent expressions, Rose currently designs over forty new dolls a year, conducts seminars, and is working on a "how - to" book on sculpting. She has two new companies, *Rose of Sharon*, which manufactures miniature figurines of mythology characters and *Little Darlins* which sells molds of her designs.

9

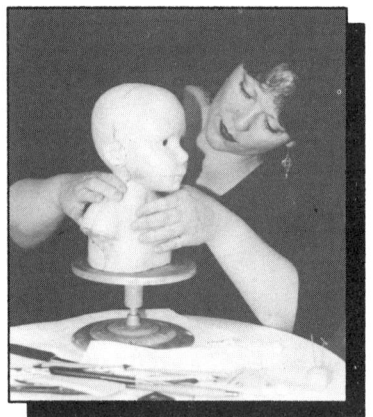

Julia Rueger is the talented artist behind *Julia Rueger LTD.* of Crestline, CA. A former certified ceramics teacher, Rueger turned to porcelain dollmaking in 1982. She is best known for her fresh-faced children with vibrant costumes. Rueger dolls have custom made armatures and range in size from 14 to 28 inches. They are limited to small editions of 45 or fewer. The artist also introduced a new line of resin dolls in 6 and 22 inch sizes.

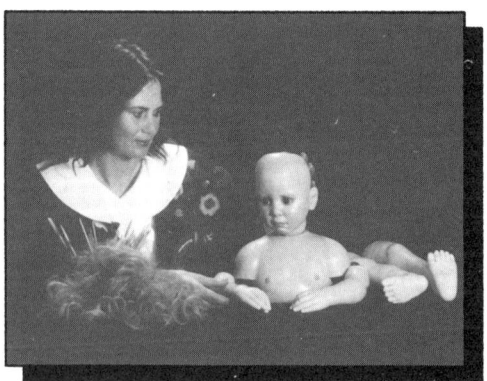

Rotraut Schrott lives and works in Baldham, Germany, where she produces 30 inch one-of-a-kind, life-like children in Cernit. *The Great American Doll Company* reproduces some of her portrait dolls and artist designs in vinyl and porcelain signed limited editions. This award-winning artist, whose treasured pieces adorn the finest museums, also authored the book titled, *Making Original and Portrait Dolls in Cernit*.

10

Pat Secrist, of *Johannes Zook Originals*, a division of *Secrist Toys, Inc.* Midland, MI, sculpts the dolls while his wife Joanna designs them. Produced in both porcelain and vinyl, the lines include children and babies from a variety of ethnic backgrounds. The company also offers three related product lines and are currently the only manufacturer of acrylic doll eyes in the U.S. today.

FayZah Spanos of *Precious Heirloom Dolls* in Tarpon Springs, Florida, entered the doll world by reconstructing old dolls. Her first original porcelain dolls appeared in 1991. She is best known for her realistic life-like 22 to 24 inch baby and toddler dolls, produced in both porcelain and vinyl. The artist sells her molds and has designed several smaller series dolls for the *Danbury Mint Company.*

Sherry Stephens, of *Best Wishes by Sherry Stephens*, entered the doll world with a Masters of Fine Arts Degree. Known for her angel-faced 12 inch porcelain babies and cherubs, each doll carries the trademarked *crossed fingers.* Her work is represented by *Doll Makers Originals International.* Stephens also teaches art for an international baccalaureate middle school magnet program.

Ruth Treffeisen, of Wiggensbach, Germany, known for the thought provoking expressions on her one-of-a-kind and limited edition dolls, just celebrated her 11th year as a dollmaker. Treffeisen's dolls range from 15 to 32 inches and are produced both in fine porcelain and vinyl. The artist also launched a line of high quality doll clothes and accessories.

Susan Wakeen, the award winning artist behind *The Susan Wakeen Doll Company* of Canton, CT, is best known for her "peaches-and-cream" babies and toddlers, boasting a healthy mid-western look. Averaging in size from 17 to 21 inches, Wakeen produces both porcelain and vinyl dolls. She also designed a series of dolls for *The Danbury Mint Company.*

Nancy Walters, of Longwood, Florida, has been sculpting one-of-a-kind dolls in a variety of media since 1986. She is one of a few artists who sculpt directly in porcelain clay. Her sculpting style is light caricature. Subjects range from literary to fantasy to ordinary people, usually elderly and often interpreted in a humorous manner. She was elected to the *National Institute of American Doll Artists* in 1991.

G. F. (Fritz) Wolff, of *The Wimbledon Collection*, Lexington, Kentucky, first entered the doll scene in 1970, producing lower end market dolls. In 1992, the sculptor launched a very affordable line of limited edition designer dolls, *The Designer Series Original Sculptures*, sculpted exclusively by Wolff and his daughter Gretchen Wolff (pictured above with her father). Recently the company began producing a full line of all-porcelain, 12 inch *Pocket Dolls*.

Chapter Two

GETTING STARTED

As a writer in the doll industry, I have spent years interviewing many of today's top doll artists. They have graciously allowed me to delve into their professional and personal lives, asking the questions collectors and aspiring doll artists wonder about most often. Top on the list is how each of these individuals actually got started in the dollmaking business. What twist of fate or act of destiny set their feet on the paths of dollmaking? Many answers appear as simple as the love of dolls while others prove as complex as the art itself. Yet, with these answers we gain a greater insight into the characters of today's most successful doll artists.

WHAT GOT YOU STARTED IN THE DOLLMAKING BUSINESS?

FayZah Spanos: "Since I was a little girl, I've always been interested in art. I worked with anything I could get my hands on. My friends still tease me about taking clippings from sponges off the fishing docks and carving little ducks and swans out of them. Gradually, I began making all sorts of crafts to sell on the docks or at craft shows.

"One day I saw a sign for an estate sale and stopped in to see what they had. I found an entire room filled with old dolls and made an offer for half the lot! My husband thought I was crazy because they just looked like old junk to him, but I thought that I could fix them up and sell them with my crafts. I did, and it worked out so well that I bought more junk dolls. I'd take parts from three broken dolls and piece together one perfectly good doll. By the time I got through they looked like new one-of-a-kind porcelains. Soon after that I tried making reproductions dolls and kept thinking that I could probably do even better if I sculpted my own. At first it was a real challenge to work with the clay, but once I tried it I knew that's what I was meant to do."

◆ ◆ ◆

Paul Cress: "It all started as a hobby, really. Peter and I met working set and costume design in the theater. About that same time I began fooling around with a styrofoam/plaster of paris sculpture of Marlene Dietrich, my all time favorite actress. I made the form into a doll and to my surprise, it sold. So, we simply made some more. It all just sort of grew into a dollmaking business from there."

16

◆ ◆ ◆

Janet Ness: "I never intended on being an artist. All of my schooling and background was in science. I worked very hard for a long time to become a scientist, but I just kept thinking that there had to be more. After my marriage I used my art minor to get into a graphics and design business that I ran out of my home.

"One day I spotted a porcelain Santa Claus in a Neiman Marcus store and just fell in love with it, only I didn't have the money to buy him. I figured it couldn't be that hard to make one myself, so I decided to give it a try. I enrolled in a porcelain dollmaking class only to end up arguing with the teacher about how he thought I should do things. Soon he learned to just ignored me and let me do it my own way. My first successful doll, Lucy 1927, was sculpted as a tribute to my mom from a picture of her as a young girl. Lucy was such a success that I decided to keep making dolls."

◆ ◆ ◆

Jan McLean: "I made my first doll for my daughter in 1983. When her friends saw it, they all wanted me to make dolls for them as well. I had been a potter for five years and had gained a knowledge of kilns and clays and glaze. I learned dollmaking as I taught others.

"I brought some dolls to my first New York Toy Fair, during the middle of the Gulf War, which was very frightening. We had left summer in the Pacific and arrived to a hard New York winter. We were babes in the woods. The huge box with all my dolls was missing and the local bank wouldn't give us American dollars. We had to drive all around New York City

17

in a cab, looking for a bank that would exchange New Zealand dollars. We were unfamiliar with tipping - but learned very quickly. After finally locating our dolls, we arrived at the Javitts Center and were totally overwhelmed by the amazing displays of toys and dolls. We absolutely panicked because all we brought to display my dolls was a white pleated table cloth. Horrors! We frantically looked around town for flowers to decorate our booth, but they were so expensive because it was winter and they had been imported from Europe. Crestfallen, we staggered back through the snow in tears, doomed to failure - or so we thought. Before our dolls were even unpacked, they were all sold. And that's how it all started. A miracle."

◆ ◆ ◆

Julia Rueger: "I grew up in Arizona near a large Indian reservation, so I was used to seeing beautiful things created from earthenware. All through school I was an advanced art student and loved dolls. Years later, I began taking ceramics classes as a hobby and enjoyed them so much that I went on to become a certified ceramics teacher. I also attended fine-arts classes to supplement my art education and learned to handle china paints. It wasn't long, however, before I outgrew ceramics. I think porcelain was a natural progression for me.

"I started by painting little hearts and balloons on the cheeks of reproduction dolls and clowns. Then I dressed them up in original costumes. I took some of these to my first doll show in 1981. They sold really well. After many, many doll shows, I decided to get serious and try an original sculputre."

◆ ◆ ◆

Fritz Wolff: "I started out in 1968 quite by accident. I was teaching a sculpting course at a local college, when a student of mine approached me and asked if I would help him make the head of a doll for his daughter for Christmas. Frankly, I was a little annoyed at first, but I agreed to help. To my surprise, I found that I really enjoyed it and began sculpting dolls for my own girls as well. At the time I owned a chain of retail gift shops and thought to sell some of my dolls with the other merchandise. They were such a success that within a few years I left the retail business completely and began mass producing the dolls in our factory overseas."

◆ ◆ ◆

Kathy Barry-Hippensteel: "I've had this crazy doll fetish since I was a kid. I think it's like a disease that you're born with. Love dolls and you'll love them all your life. To tell you the truth, there was a time in my life when dolls were the only thing that kept me going. They were my friends, my comfort, my incentive. When I no longer had the money to buy new ones, all I could think of was finding a way to get more dolls.

"One day I saw a sculpting class and thought, 'there's an idea. I'll just make my own dolls so I won't have to buy them.' I got permission to reproduce my favorite vinyl baby doll in porcelain. Then I went out and spent my last penny on a small kiln and a tiny advertisement in a national magazine. I got 400 orders and immediately turned around and did the same thing with another doll. I eventually tried sculpting my own."

◆ ◆ ◆

Ruth Treffeisen: "Childhood memories of the post-war times, today's cool reality and the retirement from my profession due to health reasons, has awakened in me the need and desire to create something beautiful and lovely. For me, the fascination in making dolls lies in its variety, which makes it possible for a dollmaker to express oneself in crafts as well as art."

◆ ◆ ◆

Julie Good-Kruger: "My special hobby as a child was my antique doll collection. I researched the dolls and gave talks about them to Brownie and 4-H groups from the time I was ten years old. While I was finishing up college and trying to figure out how I could pay for graduate studies in classical archaeology, I had a dream one night that I was making dolls. I woke up and thought, 'why not?' I never was able to set enough money aside to go to graduate school before I became a mom and had too many other responsibilities, but I have continued to work in dollmaking without regrets. This year is the nineteenth year that I have been making dolls, and I've now sold them commercially for sixteen."

◆ ◆ ◆

Hildegard Gunzel: "I saw a beautiful doll collection at a friends house and liked it so much that I decided I wanted my own collection. From there I decided to make my own dolls as well."

◆ ◆ ◆

Maggie Iacono: "Cloth has always been my thing. My mother taught me to sew when I was very little and I've always sewn my own cloths. In 1981, my sister showed me a book on how to make cloth dolls. That's really what piqued my interest in dollmaking. I thought it would be a good way to earn some extra money, so I started making sort of a rag doll, more of a play type doll, to sell at craft shows. The response was very good. Then

20

someone told me about doll shows, which I knew nothing about, . and I started doing those. At one of these shows I saw John Wright's dolls and it all just clicked for me. I always wanted a more realistic looking doll with a three dimensional face. When I saw his work, I thought it had a great blending of cloth with a sculptured face. That was the turning point for me."

◆ ◆ ◆

Cindy McClure: "I wanted to start a doll collection for my four daughters, something they would cherish and hand down through the generations. I had no intentions of making dolls until after attending my first doll show. I was so taken back at the cost of some of the dolls and knew that buying them was out of my financial capabilities at the time. Then one of the ladies selling dolls at the show told me that she had taken classes to learn how to make them. I figured that if she could learn to make dolls, so could I. I took few classes to learn the basics, which was just the right amount of kindling to start the fire.

"At that time there were only a handful of artists who were sculpting their own dolls. Very little literature was available. Actually I couldn't find any, which was probably to my benefit. It was easy to logically pick up some clay, then think through the next step. If I knew how difficult it was going to be all at one time, I may never have struggled through my first piece!"

◆ ◆ ◆

Pat Secrist: "Actually, we intended to open a small toy shop and offer a line of hand made toys. We decided to start with dolls, though *Barbie* was the extent of our knowledge of dolls at the time. We got out the yellow pages, found some doll shops, and started asking how we could make those little plastic dolls. Nobody seemed to know, but they suggested that we try porcelain dolls. We'd never heard of porcelain other than for plates, but we found a company who made porcelain dolls and they told us what books to buy. We just went home and followed them.

"I had some art background, so I sculpted my daughter and then made a mold of it according to the book. I soon found out that the books don't tell you everything. But I succeeded somehow in making a usable mold. I cast it in porcelain, put it in my little kiln, fired it for the first time in my life, and promptly burned a big hole in our carpet. That's how we got started. We never did open that little toy shop."

◆ ◆ ◆

**Rotraut Schrott**: "I learned to draw and paint from my father, Ludwig Adam, a well-known artist. Later I sculpted little animals and figures with my three children. I liked this very much. I read an advertisement for a dollmaking class and decided to do this. With the first lesson I felt immediately that this was my life and my way. In 1980, I surprised my mother with a self-sculpted doll for Christmas. Those simple lessons motivated me to begin and never to stop creating dolls."

◆ ◆ ◆

**Wendy Lawton**: "Dolls have always been an important part of my life from the day that the first baby doll was placed in my arms, when I was less than a year old. All of my childhood memories seem to feature one doll or another. Even as a teen-ager, _Barbie_ fascinated me. In the early years of my marriage I checked books out of our library on dollmaking and experimented with all kinds of different media - cloth, plaster, even bread dough. It was when

I discovered porcelain dollmaking that I knew I had found my media. I began making porcelain portrait dolls in 1979, first as a hobby, then later by commission. The *business* of making dolls grew out of that."

◆ ◆ ◆

Patricia Rose: "I was first inspired to make dolls six years ago while visiting an art shop owned by some friends. I was spellbound by a porcelain doll made by Marilyn Radzat. I had worked as a portrait artist for twenty years and found it a real challenge making the transition from working in two dimension to three dimensional dolls. It took about a year of creating little creatures that looked like *E.T.* before I achieved a point where I considered them appealing and salable."

◆ ◆ ◆

Jerri McCloud: "I had no intentions of getting into dolls because I knew nothing about dollmaking. I taught ceramics classes. We made little ornaments to sit around our homes. One day I signed up for a porcelain seminar thinking that it was a stronger medium to use for crafts. You really have to give porcelain a good whack to break it. A small segment of the seminar dealt with dollmaking. Once I saw it done, I knew I could do it. When I got back home, I became a porcelain dealer and went all out learning to sculpt dolls.

"Back then there weren't dollmaking studios like today and there certainly weren't any books out. I had to learn by myself through trial and error. I just kept at it and didn't stop at any road blocks until I had learned. Soon I was out straight working day and night producing dolls until I was ready to drop. Jim and I talked about it and decided that we couldn't go on like that. I either had to scale way back on the dollmaking, or go forward full force. It was a now or never situation, but we felt that we owed it to ourselves to give it a shot. And we did."

◆ ◆ ◆

Sherry Stephens: "For 20 years I worked as a commercial artist involved in every aspect of industrial, interior, and graphic design and loved it. I had three boys so all I'd been looking at for the past 15 or 20 years was little G.I. Joes and other boy toys. I'd forgotten all about dolls until I saw a Sonja Hartmann piece in a local shop window. Something about her struck me. I just had to have her. She was what inspired me to sculpt portraits of my boys. Later that year, when my mother became seriously ill, I decided to sculpt a 12-inch doll to cheer her up rather than just send flowers. The doll turned out so well, that I decided to develop a whole line of them."

◆ ◆ ◆

Floyd Bell: "I am a wood shop teacher. In 1978, I carved a doll to show my students how to make something of real value from scraps of wood. The result was a tall willowy peg-legged lady that they all loved and played with every day. I enjoyed making her so much that I kept making more. My early dolls sat around my house without any clothes on until my wife, Sandra, met Doris Parker, an expert seamstress, who agreed to trade clothes for dolls!"

◆ ◆ ◆

Uta Brauser: "As a child I grew up watching my mother express her artistic talents in many ways. People would come to our home for her to do their portraits and I would help her by giving my opinion. By age eleven I was sketching and painting portraits too.

I was sixteen when I sculpted a marionette portrait of my friend for his birthday surprise, and dressed it in the typical clothes he wore at the time. I also did his brother as a marionette and put on a little show at their birthday party. After I saw how striking a portrait could be as a whole figure, I kept making them and eventually began doing dolls as well."

◆ ◆ ◆

Karen Blandford: "After high school I got a job as a painter for the railway. I was the first woman ever to be apprenticed by the State Rail Authority in that trade. I painted the carriages and did a bit of sign writing, which was the reason I took the apprenticeship. I wanted to attend art school but we needed the money, so I had to take a job instead. While I was on holiday, I passed by a ceramics shop that displayed several dolls in the window. When I found out that the shop offered classes in dollmaking, I signed up right away. Before I knew it, I enjoyed making dolls more than I enjoyed my job and took more time off work to attend more dollmaking classes. I was hooked. Eventually, I found that I had too many dolls and that selling them would be necessary if I wanted to keep making them. It just grew from there."

◆ ◆ ◆

Marilyn Bolden: "I studied to be a fashion designer but I realized that I just didn't have the personality to go off to New York and showcase myself to all the world. I got married and had babies instead.

"I used to buy cloth dolls for my daughter when she was little, but found that they tore apart too easily when she played with them. My mother and I decided to make more durable cloth dolls and animals.

"One day, while waiting in a doctor's office I saw a doll magazine featuring artist dolls. I was shocked because I knew nothing about the doll world. As I read that magazine, I realized for the first time that people like me could actually make dolls like that at home! It was very exciting. I bought some clay and started working with it. I was surprised to discover how much I really enjoyed it and that I seemed to sculpt so well. Through trial and error, I pieced together an acceptable portrait doll and decided to place a small ad in a doll magazine just to see what would happen. That's how I got started on one-of-a-kind Sculpey portrait dolls. After doing that for a while, I tried the porcelain limited editions dolls, which is where I am now."

◆ ◆ ◆

Wee Paulson: "Because of a heart condition, I grew up a semi-invalid which gave me an opportunity to have a lot of free time on my hands. That's really when I started to make things out of whatever was on hand, just to keep busy. I guess it became a habit because I still do. We didn't have craft shops back then, so I had to forage for all my own materials. When my children were growing up, I created story book scenes with all the characters and everything. For my daughter I did *Little House in the Big Woods* from Laura Ingles Wilder's series. I made the house, the woods, Ma, Pa, and all the kids and I liked it so much I've been doing little scenes ever since."

◆ ◆ ◆

Susan Wakeen: "Art was always a part of my life because my father was an artist. I was constantly asking him to help me draw pictures of my dolls. I've always loved children. They are my favorite subjects. After I got married I wanted to try sculpting but couldn't find a sculpting teacher. I did find a woman who taught reproduction doll making though. After making just a few repro-

26

ductions, I decided to do my own sculptures! I made my first original doll in 1982."

♦ ♦ ♦

Nancy Walters: "Dollmaking was the result of my mid-life crisis. My first careers included teaching, advertising, and then instructional development; by the mid '70s, I was doing free-lance training materials full time and quite content. After moving to Florida with a traveling husband and two young daughters, losing my local free-lance contacts along the way, I decided to try the "mommy track." Luckily, through a pre-school bazaar, I found something to save my sanity - I began making bread dough orna-ments. After selling these at local craft shows for a couple of years, I realized it didn't make much sense to get as complicated and detailed as I was, working in a medium that could be eaten by bugs. Clay seemed the appropriate choice in terms of perma-nency. By the mid 1980s, I had become the (self-described) *Queen of Cute Clay* in central Florida, making everything from pudgy angels to hatching dragons.

"Then I decided to try decorative clay hand puppets. Elation at doing something different prevented me from seeing just how bad they were. I cranked out witches, wizards, baying bassets and sanguine santas and left the body parts laying on the shelf, because I had know idea how to put them all together.

"During a trip to New Orleans, I happened upon a doll show and discovered *art dolls*. There were over a dozen Van Craigs which completely floored me; I simply couldn't believe that such outrageous and exciting dolls existed. When I got back home, I immediately threw out the previously sculpted heads and body parts and completed five fine-grained stoneware rod puppets. However, I still hadn't figured out how to make a successful body or a doll. Knowing that I didn't want a simple "cookie cutter" cloth body, I experimented with a variety of approaches. I finally achieved a body that was adequate for my work at the time. I was not aware of dollmaking magazines at all, so I kept reinventing wheels. After working in a vacuum for about 18 long, frustrating months, the transition from cute clay to dolls was complete."

♦ ♦ ♦

Maggie Iacono

Chapter Three

THE STUDIO

Let's face it, for most of us the idea of peeking into a successful artist's private studio is a very intriguing thought, for within these rooms creativity takes shape and gives birth to new ideas. It is only natural that those of us outside the closed doors of these inner sanctums should wonder what they look like inside. The truth is, even most doll artists are curious about other artist's studios. To satisfy that curiosity and help us better visualize where and under what circumstances our favorite artists create the dolls we love, I have asked the dollmakers to open up their studios and tell all. The answers are as varied as the artists themselves and reveal much about their attitudes and personalities.

HOW WOULD YOU DESCRIBE YOUR STUDIO?

**Uta Brauser**: "I moved my studio to New York because the people here are so open to contact and that is very important to me as an artist. The studio itself is the typical New York loft, very industrial with high ceilings and 1,250 square feet of floor space. I live in a small space in the back corner. There is an airbrush room, a ten foot by ten foot showroom, a corner for sculpting, an assembling and storage area, and a shipping station. I also have two industrial sewing machines and large tables for cutting fabric. Everything I need is right here. Sometimes I see weeks fly by and I have no idea what's happened on the outside."

◆ ◆ ◆

**Sherry Stephens**: "I work all over the house including the kitchen, where I have these mini work stations set up all across my counter like a factory assembly line. I couldn't imagine doing this in a separate studio because it's so nice to work right here, where I can make my dolls and dinner at the same time. My sewing machine is set up in the bedroom, but when I have hand sewing to do, I just sit on the couch and sew while I watch television. I sculpt whenever and wherever it's quiet and I can concentrate on what I'm doing. I love working at home, but sometimes it gets short on space, though. Like right now my bathtub is full of packing peanuts and bubble wrap!"

◆ ◆ ◆

FayZah Spanos: "My studio has always been in my garage. In the evenings after everybody has gone to sleep or during my spare time on the weekends, I slip in there and have the most peaceful time. Everything I need is right there and I can create as much mess as I want without worrying about it messing up the showroom or my house. I've got my water, my table with all my clays, and all my tools spread out ready to use. I just go in there whenever I can and get started right away. The great part is I don't have to clean up after each time. I can leave everything right where it is and know that it won't be disturbed until I get back to it. It's wonderful, really."

◆ ◆ ◆

Peter Coe: "Our main workshop is located at the top of the house in the attic. It's not ideal, always hitting ones head against the sloping ceilings, and it's always a dump. There is very little room to maneuver. The cabinets and chests are nearly all collapsing with the weight of the fabrics and our research material such as books and videos. Our filing cabinets, full of patterns and cuttings, are bursting with information overload. Molds are stored in every available cupboard and storage area.

"The wax pouring and cleaning takes place in a recently built addition to the side of the house. It's mainly just a covered passageway that is externally plumbed and wired to accommodate my industrial melter." (The artists have recently bought an old dairy and plan to renovate it as their new studio.)

◆ ◆ ◆

Wee Paulson: "I live in a small one bedroom apartment so I don't have much room. I make all the dolls on my large kitchen table under a 200 watt bulb. There are boxes and boxes all over the place filled with stuff that I've been collecting for over 35 years. I keep the boxes close by when I work, because I just never know what I'm going to need to use or what special touch I'll want to add. I have a lot of friends who sometimes drop in to chat, but they all know me well enough to just step over the boxes."

◆ ◆ ◆

Karen Blandford: "My studio is detached from the house out in the back yard. It isn't exactly tidy, perhaps *organized chaos* would describe it best. However, it is light and airy because I like to work with the doors and windows open. The walls are lined with shelves for molds and greenware. I have a couple of tables where I pour greenware and a bench under the windows where I do just about everything else. I have a television and a compact disk player to keep me amused and my two dogs for company. Little Pee-Wees, native Australian birds, often come in to visit me while I work. They sometimes get only a foot or two away, stealing bits and pieces of the dog's food. I'm planning on having a verandah built off the studio, which I will cover with vines, so that I can work outside in nice weather."

◆ ◆ ◆

Wendy Lawton: "My studio is on our farm in a restored 1902 tank house. The studio is on the bottom floor with thirteen foot ceilings. I have floor to ceiling bookcases on the east wall, filled to overflowing with my collection of children's illustrated books, along with reference books and my collection of National Geographics dating back to 1922. A library ladder slides along the crown molding. On the south wall I have floor to ceiling doll cases, housing one of each doll that Lawtons has issued (over 130 so far). There is a French door in the midst of the doll cases which leads out to my rose garden. Behind my work table, on the west wall, I have drawers and cubbies sheltering all the "stuff" of dollmaking. On the north wall, to my left side as I sit at my worktable, is a window facing my kitchen garden."

◆ ◆ ◆

Rotraut Schrott: "I live with my family in Baldham, Germany, in a big wonderful house in the midst of greenery. From the living-room you can go upstairs to the gallery. It is a large bright room with a big window. In the morning the sun shines into it. This is the most tremendous time for me to sculpt. I look into my garden (like a park) with big old oak trees. Very often the squirrels are running up and down the trees, and the birds are singing in the branches. On such a wonderful day I find myself very motivated to sculpt my dolls and to bring deep feelings and sensitivity into their faces.

"The room itself is very crowded with all of the things I need. There are many shelves with fabrics, shoes, hats, paper flowers, and tools. In the midst of all this I have my table and chair where I work. Scattered around the table and on the floor, are all the things I need at that moment (tools, colors, material, doll parts). When I create the dresses for my one-of-a-kind dolls, all the laces, fabrics, ribbons, and other treasures are around me and the doll so that I can test what looks best on her. When the days are rainy and dark, many lamps are fixed around my work-table to bring day-light into my studio, I also use them to work late into the night.

"My desk is in front of the window. On it are my phone

and my fax machine, both of which make me feel connected to the whole world! I am always very happy when I work in my studio and suddenly the fax brings me a message from another continent, or the phone rings and I hear a friendly voice from far away."

♦ ♦ ♦

Cindy McClure: "Studio? What a joke! I'm sure that everyone who is or has been in this business can relate. I started in the corner of my kitchen, then migrated to the family room. Eventually, it took over the garage. I moved to a bigger house but had to add another 2,500 square feet after the dolls took over again. I now have a studio in another location, approximately the size of a small house, and have just finished building another house in hopes of accommodation the dolls for at least a bit longer than the last place. I've finally come to the conclusion that it's not possible for us dollmakers to ever have enough space. I'm sure the collectors feel the same way. They always end up needing a bigger house for all their dolls and a warehouse to store all those "precious" boxes!"

♦ ♦ ♦

Patricia Rose: "My studio is in my Florida home on an island with a beautifully inspirational view of Tampa Bay. The area is famous as "the lighting capital of the world" with storms and spectacular lightning shows almost daily. I live in a three story house with lots of porches and swings. The studio is on the ground level. It's wall to wall greenware and dolls in progress. I have one assistant, Julie Pelter. Together, she and I produce all the dolls with no outside assistance. I have a pouring area, a porcelain cleaning area, two kilns, a sewing area, and a shipping area. There is one section with tables in the shape of a box. I sit in the middle where everything is at my fingertips. We call it my command station."

◆ ◆ ◆

<u>Maggie Iacono</u>: "I've taken over one of the bedrooms in our home, but it's way too small. I have counter space on all sides with a couple of sewing machines and shelves all up and down the walls. It's really getting claustrophobic! Every little nook and cranny has got something there. Because it's so cramped I always have to keep ahead of my messes."

◆ ◆ ◆

<u>Nancy Walters</u>: "Like many others, I began working at the kitchen table. I remember the Thanksgiving we had to eat out because the kitchen table was loaded with "making stuff" and the dining room table was loaded with finished "packing stuff" and it was too cold to eat on the porch. My husband and I shared a guest bedroom/office, with an early computer, a five foot drafting table, and the beginnings of the accumulation that now inundates us. By the early 1980s we were seriously evaluating the prospects of continuing our marriage, but decided that adding on to the house would be less complicated than dividing up the community property. So I moved my studio into the former master bedroom.

"Although 11' by 15' seemed immense when it first became mine, the euphoria probably lasted all of two weeks. It has been stuffed with old department store shirt cubbies and drawer units, stacks of boxes and salvaged bubble wrap, sewing machines, a couple of work tables, and an ironing board piled high with the family mending (which will be outgrown or go out of style before being fixed), and everything I have to dump quickly from other parts of the house when company is coming.

"Following a slide program that I did for a National Institute of American Doll Artists Conference, where I revealed a little information about my organizational skills, another artist and I did a follow up program on artist's studios. Some of them were immaculate, labeled, and organized, but others reflected varying degrees of chaos. We found many common elements such as hoarding stuff, failure to replace after use, and in-home studios spewing out into other parts of the house. We also learned that artists consume remarkable quantities of delivered pizza.

"No matter how much "stuff" an artist may have, there's always something missing to finish each doll. If we're lucky, we have the right thing but then it's the wrong color. Thus we move into the kitchen to heat pots of dye on the stove or in the microwave. I have a tendency to save a mixed color in the pot until a doll is completed in case I need to use it again. It becomes particularly bad when I'm working on several dolls, each using one or more mixed colors, simultaneously for several weeks. There's paperclay in the food processor and refrigerator and porcelain clay in the pasta maker and the oven is usually full of drying paper mache body parts.

"Recently, it became evident that my studio would have to be cleaned thoroughly if I were to continue making dolls. I spent three days organizing and finding places for things that had never had homes of their own. Within a week it was nearly as bad as before. Fortunatley, I have learned to sculpt in a 6 inch square spot."

◆ ◆ ◆

__Ruth Treffeisen__: "My studio and my home are one unit. I live with my family in a three-story townhouse. As all my work on the porcelain dolls is started and finished in my house, it is very crowded. All of the molds are built and the porcelain work is done in one room. In another room, the work

36

with fabrics for the costumes is done. The dresses are de-signed in my studio, then sewn by my seamstresses in their homes. A third room is reserved for all the other work, paint-ing the faces, sewing the dolls to their bodies, dressing the dolls, and so on. I do the artistic and creative work on dolls in my private rooms, because when I work on a new doll creation, I need absolute peace and quiet. Often, I retreat to my second homeland, France. There I have the time and peace to be fully creative."

♦ ♦ ♦

Jerri McCloud: "I don't sculpt in the shop. I have a work room at home. Upstairs, in my room with many windows, I have all my research materials as well as many dolls on dis-play. It is a very comfortable room overlooking our tree-lined back yard. However, to be perfectly honest, I do most of my sculpting on the center island counter in our kitchen as it is more convenient. Most of my sculpting is done in the eve-nings and on the weekends, because I can't escape the de-mands of being involved in the production at our manufac-turing facility."

♦ ♦ ♦

Jan McLean: "My studio is best described as happy chaos. When I came back from my first *Toy Fair* in New York, in 1991, I was shell shocked and completely unprepared for overnight success. I had to plan how I was going to make 400 plus dolls in a hurry. I turned my entire two storied brick Edwardian styled home into a "factory". I built storage rooms into the roof and turned a bedroom into a pouring room. I painted in the dining room, assembled and packed in the liv-ing areas of the house, and turned the sunroom into a kiln room. That's how we lived for the first twelve months.

37

"In 1992, I purchased a small warehouse which was gradually customized to suit our needs. I also took on more staff to help with making these labor intensive dolls. I have purchased the adjoining warehouse also, to use for the messy stuff.

"At present we have an area for mold-making, another for pouring and another for assembly. There is a hat room full of gorgeous vintage hats that we reblock and decorate. Another room is full of wonderful ribbons of lustrous colors and boxes full of shoes and books. Upstairs is where all the sewing is done and where the lace and fabrics are stored. Hanging along the roof are rows and rows of handmade wooden doll chairs. There is also an area upstairs set aside for heavy machinery and for the production of teddy bears. We installed skylights along the whole length of the roof so that we have lots of natural light. I have five kilns of different sizes, plus two more at home. Finally, there is a large display area under glass for visitors to see."

◆ ◆ ◆

Janet Ness: "For me, a natural environment is very important. I think it helps with the creative process. I have 3,800 square feet in my Colorado home and my work areas are spread throughout it. I sculpt and paint in a room that looks out on a very beautiful view of the Rocky Mountains and a vast stretch of game preserve, with beautiful Ponderosa pines and oak trees. I have a full view of the western and southern skyline down to *Pikes Peak*. There is a family of foxes that I watch, lots of deer, and a mountain lion that comes walking through once and a while. When I exit my studio door, I have a nice big deck. I like to set up my sculpting out there because the natural light is so much better. I have another room just for sewing and a large area downstairs for the kiln, assembly, dressing, and shipping. It's nice to have the work areas broken up. I can find things much easier that way."

♦ ♦ ♦

Pat Secrist: "Even though we have a large dollmaking facility now, I prefer to do the sculpting at home. Basically, my
studio is a tray in front of the television. I've tried sculpting
at the table, but if there's nothing else there I get bored."

♦ ♦ ♦

Julie Good-Kruger: "It is not a picturesque place, rather a
working place in a small room off our main office. I used to
have a big, picturesque area in an old grist mill, but we needed
a more modern place for the rest of the factory with truck
docks, etc., and this location is much better for practical matters like making dolls!

"My studio looks more like an office than a studio and is
smaller that most bathrooms! It is carpeted and has tall, narrow floor to ceiling windows. It also has white cabinets, a
long counter top, two tall narrow cupboard units, and floor to
ceiling shelves. I have messages, photos, and samples of
dollmaking supplies in plastic bags stapled to the walls because I always make big messes on the counter and table.
When I clean them up, I just make more big messes. The
studio is so small that I cannot be in the middle of too many
things at a time.

"Outside our building we have a stream going by with ducks
and swans and a large pond with a gazebo and wildlife. The cor-
porate center has a paved fitness trail and walking paths around
four ponds, swings, and outdoor sculptures on a massive scale. I
look out on lots of trees and well-tended flower gardens."

♦ ♦ ♦

**Susan Wakeen**: "My studio consists of a sculpting table with lights, porcelain, vinyl and wax heads, paint brushes and all the necessary tools used for pre-production purposes. It is basically a practical and functional space. I keep an extensive file of resource materials. I have to admit that I do keep the nominations and awards there too, to remind myself that sometimes I do a pretty good job. Like most artists I am never really satisfied with a design or sculpture, but at some point, I just have to stop because I am at the deadline."

♦ ♦ ♦

**Kathy Barry-Hippensteel**: "My husband built me a beautiful studio in our new home that's bigger than my entire first apartment. I have everything I need right there, but for some reason I always end up dragging the clay onto the kitchen table. I don't know why I do that."

♦ ♦ ♦

**Floyd Bell**: "It's kind of cramped. I use my den for my office equipment, computer, fax, and I also use it for sewing, carving, and painting. Woodwork is done in my garage with machines. One of our bedrooms is used for display of my finished dolls."

♦ ♦ ♦

**Hildegard Gunzel**: "I now have a newly-built 9,000 square foot doll manufacturing plant. This new location includes an attached museum for contemporary dolls, for the public to come and see."

♦ ♦ ♦

Marilyn Bolden: "I started like most artists, in the kitchen making a mess, and it grew and grew until it was just all over the place. So my dear husband, Alex, built an addition onto our home as a studio for me. I do most all of my work back there now. But I also do a lot of the sculpting when we go on vacation. We have a cabin up in North Carolina and I take my clay up there with me."

◆ ◆ ◆

Julia Rueger: "I live in a town with only 10,000 people. My office is housed in our 3,000 square foot shop. It's fully computerized with a desk, a painting table, stereo, books and a sculpting table. I have two big windows that look out on the beautiful San Bernadino mountains and a small creekbed where nearly 20 different kinds of birds come to drink water. I leave my window open most of the time because I love to hear the birds and smell the trees when I work. I need to have a relaxed and quiet environment. That's very important to me."

◆ ◆ ◆

Fritz Wolff: "My daughter Gretchen, and I do all the sculpting for the dolls. We work independently of each other just so the dolls don't end up all looking the same. We do the wet sculpting here in Lexington. I usually do my sculpting at home on the weekends or in the evenings when it's quiet. Sometimes I have five or six heads going at the same time, all scattered across the kitchen table. I also have a large conference table here at the office that I do things on and I'll often use the time I spend on airplanes to sketch out designs."

◆ ◆ ◆

41

Wendy Lawton's Studio

Chapter Four

DAILY ROUTINE

For many of today's successful doll artists, finding enough time to work their craft proved the hardest part of starting up and maintaining a dollmaking business. In some cases, many difficult decisions and sacrifices had to be made to squeeze dollmaking into their lifestyles and budgets. But for others, dollmaking fit like a good pair of jeans. In this chapter you will learn some of the artist's time management secrets, how they work around active families, household duties, and administrative responsibilities, with enough quiet time left over for artistic expression. As they share a typical day with us, you may be surprised to learn that our favorite doll artists are creative in more ways than one.

WHAT IS YOUR TYPICAL DAILY WORK ROUTINE?

Nancy Walters: "Routine is probably necessary for great ac-
complishments and accumulation of wealth, but it's also one of the
things I avoid. Some days I work 18 hours. Some days I don't
work at all. Wednesday and Saturday are the same to me and it
often takes me a few seconds to figure out what day it actually is.
I work when I want and/or need to, and give myself plenty of
flexibility. I must admit that I occasionally get myself in a bind and
have to put in some pretty heavy weeks to meet a deadline. But
sometimes I need a bit of pressure to perform up to speed, because there are certain aspects of dollmaking that I don't care for,
such as wigging, that I will postpone until there is no tomorrow.
Sometimes I get to something on a doll that I don't want to do, so
I put it aside and work on another doll until I get to something I
don't want to do on it either. That may go on until I'm looking at
5 or 6 unfinished dolls! It's a little like living on a roller coaster, but
that strikes me as more bearable than spending life on a plane
surface.

"What is pretty constant is that I am a night person. I've always stayed up late and gotten my best work done then. Since I
no longer have to get up to get kids off to school, my usual 2 a.m.
bedtime often stretches to 3 or 4 a.m.. I have been known to
work all night when I got on a roll. So don't call me before 10
a.m.. While the rest of the east coast is breaking for lunch, I'm
just beginning my real day.

"I do need to work in reasonably long stretches of time. I
can't pick up something and work for 15 minutes or even an
hour, go to the dentist, come home and work another hour
before taking off for the grocery store. I know doll artists who

manage to accomplish amazing amounts while juggling car pools and cooking dinner, all the time with a toddler clinging to one leg; I have never been able to do that. I can write or sew human clothes in short snatches but I can't make dolls that way."

♦ ♦ ♦

Maggie Iacono: "I'm not a morning person. I usually get up between 9 and 10 o'clock. My husband gets the kids off to school so I don't have to worry about that. Then we sit down and have a cup of coffee together before we begin work. He's a big part of the business too. I couldn't do this without him. We work until school gets out, meeting with the seamstresses and doing the business end in addition to the dolls. Then, when the kids get home, I have to drop everything for half an hour or so, because they all want to tell me about their days. I try to get back to work after that and usually work until dinner. After dinner I'll work until 9 or 11 o'clock in the evening, but I don't usually go beyond that because it doesn't work for me to be tired."

♦ ♦ ♦

Jan McLean: "Every single day of the week is devoted to dollmaking and no day is ever the same. When I am not traveling to America or Europe, I start work each day at 8:30 a.m. with piles of letters, faxes, and phone calls. Then I try to settle down and work on the heads, which sometimes takes 3, 4 or 5 china firings. I mainly paint in the evenings though, because I get too many interruptions during the day. I am not just a dollmaker now, I am first a business woman, then a dollmaker.

"I have a wonderful team of workers. Without them I would not be as successful. Nobody can produce this much all on their own because the dolls are so special and labor intensive and completely made by hand. We work until at least 12 o'clock every evening. Sometimes my dressmaker and I stay until 5 am to work on a costume for a new doll. We have peace and quiet then and can spend hours draping and playing. At the end of every week we assemble and dispatch the dolls, all of which I oversee. I have a "treasure" who comes to my home every day for 2-3 hours to run my household and cook our meals. Every woman needs a wife! If I didn't have her, I would find life very difficult.

"When busy people work such long hours, it is also very important to make time for others. I am very aware of this and have to juggle my life to make time for family and friends. I am so lucky to have such a supportive husband. My children are grown up and living in different parts of the world, so I get to see them on my travels. If I had a young family, none of this would be possible for me."

♦ ♦ ♦

**Peter Coe**: "It's actually quite dreary, really. If we're not in America selling, we're at home working seven days a week, ten to twelve hours a day. We enjoy our work, but it is quite tiresome at times. And of course a great deal of our time goes into pouring over research materials. We also visit as many museums and art galleries as we possible can."

♦ ♦ ♦

**Wendy Lawton**: "Unfortunately, there never seems to be a typical day. I have to balance my time between solid blocks of creative time, manufacturing responsibility and administrative tasks. In addition, the work is sandwiched between periods of travel and/or visitors and tours.

"On a day when I've planned to be working in my studio (as opposed to going in to town to work at Lawtons), I usually spend the early part of the morning gardening (when I am least focused). I start working mid-morning and work until school is out. I usually take time out with the kids and prepare dinner. Then I am back out to the studio after dinner and work until I am "at a place" (meaning a good place to stop or finished with a certain task). This is usually sometime after midnight."

♦ ♦ ♦

Wee Paulson: "I'm kind of a 24 hour person. I don't have enough sense to go to bed at night. But that's the neat thing about being old (69) I can make my own hours. I don't work five days a week. I work a little bit each day when I feel like it."

♦ ♦ ♦

Patricia Rose: "Since my studio is in-home, there is no escape from work. Work starts at 8 a.m. when my assistant arrives. Now that most of my work is planned months in advance, I'm able to finish at around 5 p.m. The day's first half is a rush to complete dolls for shipping. Later, I sculpt, paint, sand or detail greenware, or pour porcelain for future orders. Then I finish the day by firing the kiln. I'll often slip back down stairs in the evenings to sculpt while all is quite."

♦ ♦ ♦

Susan Wakeen: "There is no typical day for me as every day has a new set of challenges. When we are preparing for a big show, my day starts at 4 o'clock in the morning. I sculpt until 7 o'clock and then have breakfast with my husband/

47

business partner. We then go into the factory to make sure everything is running smoothly. Some days I stay all day for support or to troubleshoot. Other days are filled with planning meetings and "what to do about" meetings. Because I choose to remain involved in every aspect of the production of the dolls, I don't spend nearly as much time as I'd like to on designing, although I am trying to change that."

◆ ◆ ◆

Julia Rueger: "I enjoy having some time to myself in the morning. I tend to a few chores around the house and throw dinner in the crock pot before I leave. I'm usually at the shop by 9 a.m. and stay until between 5 and 7 p.m. I used to go there every day and night, but I've found that I just can't do that anymore. I need to spend some time at home puttering around the house doing laundry and all that normal stuff. So, I'm trying to free up some time by not going in on Sundays or staying late at night. And I don't bring work home unless it's just simple needle work. My routine at work varies from day to day. Some days I'm painting, some days I'm cleaning greenware, and somedays I'm assembling."

◆ ◆ ◆

Jerri McCloud: "We employ 30 workers at the manufacturing facility. I'm there five days a week, eight to ten hours a day, because I can't escape the demands of being involved in production. Even though Jim oversees most of it, I still have to have a hand in. I can't let go, or let's put it this way, I won't let go. My office is at the end of the production line, so before anything goes out, it passes by me first. We do manage to take some time off on the weekends though."

◆ ◆ ◆

Kathy Barry-Hippensteel: "I have five children, two older daughters, a two and a half year old girl and one year old twins (a girl and a boy), so basically my daily routine consists mostly of babies right now. I wake up every morning to babies. When the babies go down for their naps, I quickly run in and do some sculpting or painting until they wake up. So my day alternates from real babies to pretend ones. It's a non-stop thing. I'd like to say that on the weekends I spend more time on the dolls when my husband is home to help with the kids, but I don't because I want to spend that time with him! That's just the way it is right now and that's why my sculpting is limited to the *Ashton Drake Galleries* at this time. But I do have this huge hope chest full of ideas, that I will try to get to someday, hopefully before I croak! Till then, I'll just keep plodding along doing the best I can with the time I have."

◆ ◆ ◆

FayZah Spanos: "Dollmaking occupies almost every aspect of my life. Next to my family, it is my whole life. If I'm relaxing, I'm reading a doll magazine. If I'm out to dinner with my husband, we're talking about dolls. We are at the shop everyday, but we bring our son there with us as much as possible. At night when everyone else is asleep, I go off into my own little world and sculpt. It's sometimes very tiring but I love every minute of it."

◆ ◆ ◆

Hildegard Gunzel: "I am so busy with shows and tours, but I do not let them cut into my creative time because I am very strict about when I will allow myself to create. I do not create on the road, for example, I only collect ideas then. I also never create in my studio because I have maybe 20 or 30 calls a day that interrupt my work, and I have not the patience to work with these interruptions. I do the business work at the studio

49

from 8:30 a.m. to anywhere from 6-8 p.m., and I do my creative work when I am on holiday in Spain. We have a place there where we go three or four times a year. Then I can relax and work on the ideas that I have collected and saved for this time."

◆ ◆ ◆

Cindy McClure: "I'm up at 7:00 a.m. each morning. As soon as the girls leave for school, I access my "to do" list and usually start work with phone calls. I call my sub's to make sure all is well (of course if all were well I'd be worried), then I spend most of my time sculpting, creating concepts and going back and forth to my mold makers.

"I do travel a lot, which is the frosting on the cake for me. Meeting the collectors is an experience that makes everything worth while. These people have a part of me in their lives and they are as excited to meet me as I am to meet them!"

◆ ◆ ◆

Fritz Wolff: "I live my life on an airplane! I do about thirty shows a year so I'm all over the continental United States and Canada. Three or four times a year we travel from the studio here in Lexington, Kentucky, to our factory in the Middle East. So, that means circling the globe about eight times just on those trips. We also do private appearances for doll stores to meet the public and do signings. I am virtually home, sleeping in my bed at my residence, less than six months out of the year. It's a way of life I guess."

◆ ◆ ◆

Ruth Treffeisen: "I do not like any kind of work routine. Everything that becomes a routine, hinders artistic expression. Personally, I am a night person and work very often until quite late into the night."

♦ ♦ ♦

Janet Ness: "I ran a commercial graphics-design business out of my home before getting into dolls, so I already pretty much knew how to handle the daily business end of dollmaking. I work regular business hours at it. But sculpting doesn't get scheduled. It just happens. Those special creative moments find themselves. When they do, I have to drop everything else and go with the feeling. That's what I call my golden moment - a time for me when everything is right with the universe, everything comes together and makes sense. I lock myself up in the studio, let my creative feelings go and get totally involved in the subject I am sculpting. Then it's back to the business of designing and dollmaking."

♦ ♦ ♦

Julie Good-Kruger: "I have no typical day. I juggle work for my own company, Ashton-Drake, business travel and being a wife and mother. Almost every day is different and each time of the year finds me involved in different aspects of the doll making business. My studio is located at our production center where my husband and I work each day. We used to spend our evenings experimenting with different mediums, but right now we are pretty focused on raising our eleven year old daughter. I try not to take my work home with me, because I don't want my daughter to resent it."

♦ ♦ ♦

Marilyn Bolden: "I work at this full time, from early morning until at least mid-night each day. Of course, when you work at home you take time off here and there to do other things, but most of the housework I have to let go. The dishes and the laundry always pile up because I can't be away from the dolls very long. Whenever I've got free time I'll sculpt. Usually that's late at night when all is quiet. Sometimes I'll even get up from sleep to sculpt for hours."

♦ ♦ ♦

Rotraut Schrott: "In the morning I have to do the mail. In the afternoon, evening and night I work on my dolls or do the buying of materials and fabrics. Most of the day I am in my studio creating my dolls. I sculpt them without any mold, only with my hands. It takes much more time but it brings so much more pleasure to me."

♦ ♦ ♦

Floyd Bell: "I'm up at 6:00 a.m. to teach woodworking at Westchester High School. At 2:00 p.m. I'm usually free enough to read and answer correspondence. At 4:00 p.m. I go to the woodshop again to cut out wood parts for my carved dolls. At 6:00 p.m. I meet with the doll seamstress. Then I work at home in my office/studio in the evenings."

♦ ♦ ♦

Karen Blandford: "I pretty much work seven days a week. On a usual day, I'll start work between 8:00 and 9:00 o'clock in the morning, have a break at lunch time for around an hour, and work until 5:00 or 6:00 o'clock in the afternoon, depending of who's cooking dinner! Most evenings I work from 7:30 'til 9:30 or 10:30. I don't have set days for doing things, but if I have to pour greenware or clean, I like to do it all day. I tend to sculpt during the quiet evening hours when I am more relaxed. The daylight hours are filled with too much "real" work. Sculpting comes easier and I find myself doing a better job if I wait for the bug to bite. I also do the paper work and send faxes in the evening, as the light isn't good enough for painting, cleaning, or pouring then."

◆ ◆ ◆

Sherry Stephens: "The first thing I do in the morning is get up and go for a four mile walk. While I'm walking, I do a lot of planning and thinking about what I need to accomplish the rest of the day. Then, while I'm all sweaty and messy, I usually do the dirty things like mixing up my colors or cleaning greenware. After that work is done, I'll clean up and make telephone calls and check on orders and things. I do the dollmaking right through the afternoon. The pouring and cleaning room is right next to the kitchen, so I kind of go back and forth cooking dinner in between emptying out molds and doing that kind of thing during dinner time. I can't just stand and watch the water boil, I always feel like I need to be doing two things at once.

"I really enjoy eating dinner together with my family, but after that I usually pick up some sewing or something else until it's time for bed. Of course, if I'm firing the kiln, I have to keep running out there every few hours to change the temperature and check to make sure everything goes the way it should."

◆ ◆ ◆

Pat Secrist: "We have one of the larger dollmaking companies in the United States, so we're no longer a "mom and pop" operation, which means my routine is a little different than your average doll artist. Instead of coming into a studio to push clay, I come to an office each day and take care of administrative things first. Then when I get that done, I wander around the plant and talk to the different people about what they're doing. I spend a good deal of time in our research and development department to see how we're doing on new products including dolls, doll kits, our line of eyes, and dollmaking tools. That's pretty much how I spend every day. I sculpt at home in the evenings."

◆ ◆ ◆

__Uta Brauser__: "I have no routine. Every day has different needs and schedules. Being manager of everything means there are always surprises for me to deal with. As an artist, I find the best hours are the quiet ones, late in the evening and at night. My best creations and new developments come to me most often in those undisturbed hours."

Chapter Five

IDEAS & INSPIRATION

Doll artists are creators in a very real sense. They bring into existence a new human likeness whose features and gestures mimic our own and testify of distinct, individual personalities. How many of us have looked at our dolls and wondered where the artist came up the idea for that particular theme or unusual look? What thoughts crossed their minds as they created it? How did they feel watching the medium take shape and spring to life in their hands? Do the faces they sculpt come from people they meet on the street, family photographs, or are they images from a dream? Of course, we cannot know the answers for every doll, but through this chapter we can gain a better understanding of what inspires our favorite artists as they share with us their most intimate secrets about their sources of inspiration.

55

WHERE DO YOU GET YOUR IDEAS AND INSPIRATION?

Hildegard Gunzel: "It's not as complicated as people might think. For me, coming up with the ideas is a very natural and normal process. My ideas come from everything, books, plays, drawings, art, children, people, etcetera. Sometimes I even get ideas going into the children's department of a furniture store. Where ever I am the colors, arrangements, and images just stay with me. But mostly, I think, I simply design my dreams, my own understanding of beauty."

◆ ◆ ◆

Janet Ness: "I have used images from photographs and images from people that I know, because sometimes those faces just seem to talk to me and tell me that they need to be a doll. But mostly I'll start sculpting sort of haphazardly and a face will begin to develop. Nora and Sidney did that. They're little beings in themselves. When I sit down to sculpt I get totally involved and submerged in my subject. I leave my mind completely blank to act as a sounding board, ready to catch a tone, a flash, an impression, or a spark of excitement coming from my subject. If I become too aware of myself, letting my personality get in the way, then everything falls to pieces and I never really get to the essence of the doll, which should exist with a life of its own."

◆ ◆ ◆

Jan McLean: "I really have no plan, my dolls just evolve. I get ideas from books and people in the street. Years of dedicated people watching helps, I suppose."

♦ ♦ ♦

Paul Cress: "We get our visions and inspiration from books, visits to museums, galleries, videos, history, and even music - opera in particular. Since our dolls are portraits, we want them to be as close a resemblance as possible. Therefore, a great deal of research is necessary."

♦ ♦ ♦

Karen Blandford: "Sometimes the ideas for my dolls develop as I work. Other times I'll get a clear picture of the whole thing in my mind before I begin to sculpt. Face, costume, pose, and even hair and eye color will come to me. I very rarely get an entire idea from a single source, but may occasionally be inspired by a photo or a pose I've seen. I buy a lot of bridal and fashion magazines and books on the Victorian painters, postcards, greeting cards, and movies. I use all these and just about anything else that might inspire me. Once I developed an entire doll to suit a lovely piece of inspiring fabric."

♦ ♦ ♦

Rotraut Schrott: "To sculpt portrait dolls after a living model is the biggest challenge for me. To sculpt the doll as a personality after a child, I must leave behind my own ideas and concentrate totally and completely on the child."

♦ ♦ ♦

Nancy Walters: "The hardest question anyone ever asks me about dollmaking, is where I get my ideas. I hate always sounding so vague, but I'm not really sure a lot of the time. The sources can be pretty diverse even when I can figure them out. I do know that the ideas come faster than I could possible bring them to life, even at twice my pace. Some are born in rather amorphous shape, others seem to spring into my mind almost fully developed. The fully developed ideas are the ones most likely to be put off because there doesn't seem to be much challenge. Some ideas come when I'm not really thinking about dolls, others occur from people or even events I see.

"My dolls began as and still are mostly elderly people. I have little interest in or patience with symmetry, which is necessary to create pretty, so I sculpt elderly and character dolls. When I have done younger characters, they have been gawky teen-agers or quirky fairies. Perhaps I am trying to come to grips with my own aging when I do the elderly people. Certainly I am reflecting my view of my own life when I approach most of my subjects from a humorous angle.

"Always a reader, some of my dolls come from literature, quite often books I read as a child and in which I envisioned amusing-looking characters. I enjoy another angle on the traditional treatment, which has led to the fairy tale characters revisited in later years and the 350-year-old fairies who prove that there are calories and gravity even in fantasy land. There have been a number of shopping ladies, from Sax to K-Mart, and occasionally I succumb to a little poignancy.

"What really sets me back big time is when someone whose work I revere comes up with an idea similar to one of mine and does it in a more innovative way or with greater technical skill. If I see it after I have done mine, I just cry. If I see it before, I usually can't bring myself to do the doll for a long time or maybe never."

◆ ◆ ◆

Patricia Rose: "Generally, I get my ideas and inspiration from art books. I never watch television, read the newspaper or involve myself in much else other than the art world, family and friends. I believe that not being overly concerned about what is going on in the world helps build up my creativity and allows me to maintain a positive attitude, which is in itself inspirational."

♦ ♦ ♦

Ruth Treffeisen: "I draw many of my ideas from observing and watching children at playgrounds or when I travel. All of my work is done from memory. Sometimes I see beautiful children whose faces I just soak right up, then try to recreate in clay when I get home. I always dress these children in nostalgic clothing, though I can not explain why, except that it is my preference. Old photographs of children from Europe and the United States and classical children's clothing from Italy, Spain and France are also good sources for inspirations."

♦ ♦ ♦

Kathy Barry-Hippensteel: "I don't do sweet little faces. Don't ask my why, I just can't. I like the goofy, funny little faces of babies when they're off exploring or discovering something new, or maybe getting into trouble. I really, really, enjoy babies, especially little boys. They are my inspiration. All my dolls are sculpted as boys, then Ashton Drake puts wigs on some of them and changes them into girls."

♦ ♦ ♦

Pat Secrist: "Well, I've got a pretty vivid imagination but when it comes to the faces, I'll usually look out into the population to find faces that are expressing what I'm feeling. I've

59

been known to walk up to strangers in the mall and say, 'Your child is adorable. Here's my business card. We'd like to turn her into a doll.' Or, I'll be sitting at a McDonald's and instead of a Big Mac attack I get a new face attack and run up to some parent and say, 'Your kid's great. I've got to have your kid's face.' You should see the reaction that gets! Now people are coming out of the woodwork wanting to give me their kids!"

◆ ◆ ◆

Julia Rueger: "If I had to be in any other line of work, it would probably be in textiles somehow, because I love fabrics. I definitely get ideas and inspiration for my dolls from fabrics. In fact, I pretty much pick out the fabric and then sculpt a doll to go with it. I never sketch out anything first, because I'm strictly a three dimensional artist. So, when I'm ready to sculpt, I search through my huge portfolio of children's faces to find the face or the mood or the look I'm after. Then I work from that photograph."

◆ ◆ ◆

Marilyn Bolden: "I am constantly sketching faces. It could be from a picture in a magazine or newspaper or a child that I see out on the street. I'll think, 'that's a fascinating face' and I'll go home and reproduce it on paper. I'll never run out of faces for dolls because I've got boxes filled with stacks and stacks of them. It's the same with the costumes. I just sketch out what seems right for the dolls."

◆ ◆ ◆

Sherry Stephens: "I could come up with a new doll every week if I had to. I have so many ideas and just not enough time to put them all into clay. A lot of times an artist will sculpt one doll and

60

make it into a boy and a girl, but I can't do that. Once I begin to sculpt, I already know if it's going to be a boy or a girl and no matter how it turns out, I can't put a girl wig on a boy doll.

"All of my dolls either have a dimple or a cleft chin, because that's what I'm used to looking at. Everyone in my family has one or the other or even both. Coming up with the dolls names is easy too - they're all either named after members of my family or my friends."

♦ ♦ ♦

Cindy McClure: "My ideas come mostly from my five daughters and their friends. My faces come from all over the world. I have an incredible file of pictures that have been sent to me from collectors around the world. I've always been very touched that so many people would take the time to write and send me these pictures."

♦ ♦ ♦

Floyd Bell: "Count me among the contemporary artists of today, who strive to create works of art that have universal appeal and timeless beauty. What a privilege to work with a medium I love - wood. The touch, the feel, and the smell of wood is a sensual delight in itself. To sculpt in wood is so calming and relaxing, it can be compared only to a sedative. My creations from that first doll to the *African Lady* to my *Nubian Dancer*, all give me a great sense of pride and accomplishment.

"My inspiration comes from the history of great people who contributed to the American heritage. My dolls tell a story of people from Africa who were torn from their homeland and enslaved in foreign lands. I try to capture in the faces of my dolls, the pain and suffering, the dignity and resolve of a people who endured."

61

◆ ◆ ◆

Jerri McCloud: "I've done a few portrait dolls, but I think most of my ideas come from my imagination. I like to do character dolls with a theme that depicts a moment in somebody's life, something that collectors can relate to. First I get the size of the doll in my mind, then I wait for inspiration to strike up a concept. Often one idea just leads to another. For example, I went to a book store to find a tiny book for one of my dolls and found one filled with poems. As I read them, the word 'letters' jumped out at me and I said, 'that's it, love letters!' That developed into a doll holding a bundle of love letters. So even though the poem had nothing to do with love letters, it triggered a thought. That kind of thing happens a lot. I'm kind of geared to it after twenty years now. That's just how most of my ideas are born."

◆ ◆ ◆

Rotraut Schrott: "I sculpt life-like children, very naturalistic. I love the portrait paintings of the old masters. I admire their talent to paint a face with such sensitivity, refinement, and delicate color combinations. I use their work as a pattern for me because I want my dolls to reflect this same feeling. I try to bring deep feelings and sensitivity into their faces using great expression. I also put much expression into the body-language of the dolls through the positioning of their arms and hands. This all adds to the special feelings of my dolls."

◆ ◆ ◆

Julie Good-Kruger: "I draw inspiration from my own memories of childhood, stories from my family members, observations of my own daughter, and books I have read."

◆ ◆ ◆

__Wee Paulson__: "Sometimes my inspiration can be a piece of material that I work around. Other times I might decide to work but won't quite know what I'm going to do or use, so I just dig through my boxes for shapes and things that might interest me. The piece starts to evolve from there. I get so much fun out of doing it that way.

"I find the neighborhood children to be another source of inspiration. I love to watch them from my apartment window. I'm fascinated by the things they do and some of the things they come up with. That's why I've never made two "Weedidits" the same. Why repeat a scene when there are so many wonderful scenes in life to choose from?"

◆ ◆ ◆

__Fritz Wolff__: "I start with a head and a face and a feeling, that develops into a certain type of doll. Some will go quite quickly while others I put down and let rest a week or so before I pick them up and fool with them a bit more. Then I design the clothing to go with that particular face and type of doll. Occasionally I'll work from a photograph, but usually not. Most of the time it's just a developmental type process and I don't even know what the end result is going to look like.

"After the doll is done, then I find a name. Some names fit people better than others. It's the same with dolls. We try very hard to match them up with just the right name or theme. A lot of thought goes into this."

◆ ◆ ◆

Susan Wakeen: "My ideas don't come from any one source. I start with pictures or children that project a mood or a feeling that I'd like to portray. I could be inspired by a song, a poem, or just an expression or feeling that is locked in my memory bank. Then I try to make everything that follows, dress design, hair style, coloring, or features, consistent with that feeling."

◆ ◆ ◆

Wendy Lawton: "Children's literature is my primary source of inspiration, but I also research in the areas of anthropology (for cherished customs), history, music, art, poetry, color theory, and costume."

◆ ◆ ◆

Uta Brauser: "I came to New York because New Yorkers are very open to contact, whereas I have never felt that in Paris or other large cities. This important to me as an artist because I want to feel I have open communications with the public. It's the people around me that make up my life and are my inspiration. Many of my ideas come from the people I see on the street. Observing them carefully helps me develop new themes, like my contemporary city kids or my new multi-ethnic dolls. Sometimes I'll see a person who has a certain look that I want to reproduce so I'll ask them if I can take a picture of them. I don't just see the faces though, I see the whole person. I try to understand how these people feel and sculpt those feelings into my dolls."

◆ ◆ ◆

FayZah Spanos: "At this point in my business, people expect a certain number of new faces from me each year with a certain look, and they expect each one to be better than the last. So it's a lot of pressure. All through the year I look for babies, in person or in magazines, who have a certain expression that inspires me. Then I add to their features to make them fit into my line. When I sculpt I really, really concentrate, block everything else out, and go into another world. When I'm done I look at the sculpture and wonder where in the world it came from. Then I just smile and say 'Thank you Lord," because I know it didn't come from me, only through me. The whole process is still so amazing to me, it really is."

Floyd Bell with student

Chapter Six

THE BEST SYSTEMS

Everybody has their own special way of doing things. Doll artists are no exception. I've found that in many cases their methods of operation vary as much as their dolls. One artist's "how to" book may read entirely different from another artist's book, even when working in the same medium. While the industry has definitely established time-proven right and wrong ways to work with each medium, many techniques are simply a matter of personal preference. Aspiring doll artists need to know the differences and will benefit from learning a few short cuts from the masters, while collectors will enjoy this unusual insight into the personal quirks of today's most successful doll artists.

WHAT UNIQUE METHODS OR SPECIAL SYSTEMS HAVE YOU DEVELOPED?

Sherry Stephens: "I have it worked out to where I can produce about twenty-five limited edition dolls per month by myself at home. That includes everything from sculpting to sewing. To do this I have be very organized. I don't just do one or two of anything. I guess you'd say I produce on a monthly cycle. I spend like a whole week pouring porcelain, a whole week cleaning greenware, another week painting, and the fourth week assembling. In between I'm always sewing. When I sit down and sew, I make ten or twenty outfits at a time so as not to waste time. When I finish lace for one dress, I don't cut it off and pick up the other one. I just keep everything attached into one huge, long line, and then I cut all the pieces apart when I'm done. That saves time too."

◆ ◆ ◆

Janet Ness: "One great system I discovered was putting the book work on the Quicken computer program. I put inventory and everything on it. That has just made a world of difference. Now I spend only one or two hours a week doing the bookkeeping, whereas before I'd work three times as long. It also makes my accountant and tax people very happy because it leaves a lovely, long paper trail for them to follow."

◆ ◆ ◆

Wendy Lawton: "Most of our dollmaking is about concept ideas and telling stories rather than methods and innovations. We have, however, developed a machine-method for beveling and cutting eyes, done research into the cause of "cold spots" in greenware, and invented a method for making "corn-rows" in wigging."

♦ ♦ ♦

FayZah Spanos: "My special system is the medium I use. I've used Plastiline since day one. I've tried other mediums through the years, but I haven't found anything else like it. Even though many artists "boo" it, Plastiline works for me. I'm used to it and have it down to a science now. Most of the time you'll see me running around here with a piece of it in my hand."

♦ ♦ ♦

Patricia Rose: "One unique method I have for crafting my one-of-a-kind dolls, is to mold Cernit over a porcelain skull. My preference for a particular brand of porcelain and the particular tools that I use make up my system."

♦ ♦ ♦

Floyd Bell: "I developed three techniques for wooden doll making. The first is a bandsaw cut out and join-the-pieces doll, the second is a mortise and tenon tool, and the third is with fifteen pieces, jointed and carved round."

♦ ♦ ♦

Rotraut Schrott: "I only do one-of-a-kind artist and portrait dolls sculpted directly in Cernit. My special method is to sculpt these life-like children in the same naturalistic manner as in the portrait paintings of the old masters. Their talent to paint a face with such sensitivity and delicate color combinations is an inspiration to me. I want to have my dolls reflect these same things and be seen in the same way as those great paintings."

◆ ◆ ◆

__Marilyn Bolden__: "My son Bret helps me with the dolls. He and I are both artists. As such, while we enjoy the creative aspects of dollmaking, we don't enjoy the tedium of having to do the same thing over and over - especially carving and sanding the hands and fingernails. To keep the work fresh and fun, we've worked out a schedule that allows us to be doing something different almost every day. There are a specific number of dolls that we can realistically expect to finish and ship each week. After the required number of parts are poured, I'll spend a day carving and cleaning the heads and we'll both clean the rest of the parts. After they're soft fired, I sand and refine the heads and Bret sands the rest. After the parts are hard fired we spend a day or so painting. The next several days are spent repainting, assembling, dressing and packing. This method may not be as efficient as it could be, but it works for us. We manage to meet out production goals each month and enjoy the work without getting bored."

◆ ◆ ◆

__Paul Crees__: "Our dolls are fully sculpted and anatomically correct, not a chest plate on a stuffed body. That's different. And the two tone wax is our own innovation. Technique, methods and systems are something you acquire with experience and they may change as one progresses."

◆ ◆ ◆

__Susan Wakeen__: "More than anything I feel that I've developed a style that is unique to me. I try to make my babies sweet, pretty, innocent, timeless and as "all American" as I can."

♦ ♦ ♦

Wee Paulson: "I've been saving boxes of materials for over 35 years and most of these date back to the 1930s. I've used these as a resource to draw on. Many are nice soft cottons, satins, silks and rayons, along with beautiful prints and lace trims. I always tried to influence the clothing my children bought, because I knew when they were through I'd use it again for my dolls."

♦ ♦ ♦

Julia Rueger: "I have developed a unique method for painting my freckled-faced children so that the freckles are layered with some faded and some darker. I do this by painting and firing several times before the head is completed. I feel it comes out very lifelike. I know I'm on the right track if my friend's nine year old doesn't like it!"

♦ ♦ ♦

Kathy Barry-Hippensteel: "The thing that helps me the most in my dollmaking is a positive attitude. Life is just too short to be serious. There was a time I felt like my life was all over, but it wasn't. You can look at life and cry very easily because there are so many sad things in the world. The trick is to find the good things that make you smile and that's the hardest part. I made up my mind that I'd rather be happy than sad, so I just keep this real positive attitude and use it to make happy little dolls."

♦ ♦ ♦

Hildegard Gunzel: "I use Plasteline, oil-based material, porcelain covered with special wax, and color fired into the porcelain. Those are my special methods and systems."

◆ ◆ ◆

Jan McLean: "I use only top quality fabrics, laces, trims, and wonderful people. I have twelve piece workers who custom make jewelry, shoes, furniture, and hats all to my design. I could not do this without them."

◆ ◆ ◆

Karen Blandford: "I like to use white porcelain. Then I paint over it with at least two coats of flesh color. This is an old-fashioned method though. Not a lot of people do it that way anymore, but I like it because I feel this gives a special "glow" to the skin."

◆ ◆ ◆

Uta Brauser: "I developed a method of using acrylic over porcelain. It started with ceramic and acrylic decorations. I wanted my Black kids to have this velvet look and skin texture. Porcelain seemed too smooth and cold to me. After researching, I discovered a very matte paint for the porcelain which is some sort of enamel used for painting metallic signs outdoors, but it had only synthetic colors. However, I use this paint to form a base and then I work on other acrylic or watercolors. I airbrush a lot and can do many layers of color."

◆ ◆ ◆

Julie Good-Kruger: "I don't know that I have developed any unique methods or systems except that dollmaking works better for me if I have reliable, honest, and talented co-workers. Division of responsibilities goes a long way towards improving the quality of life. I used to have to do so much more in terms of hours spent on busy work, than I do now. I have also learned to be much more organized with my time and to keep a daily calendar. That way I don't have to hold so much in my head, which frees me up to be less anxious and more creative. It also helps to have someone like my husband working by my side as a partner.

"I also spend quite a bit of time carving out the fingernails. Many people at the shows comment on how realistic the hands and nails are. It's a little thing, but it's important to me."

◆ ◆ ◆

__Pat Secrist__: "I have an engineering background so I approach everything from that standpoint. Most of my improvements or new methods are technological. For example, I invented a tool for putting on eye lashes. That job used to take an artist 20 minutes or so and that's if they didn't smear the glue all over the place. The tool that I developed alleviates that stress and turns it into a one-step operation which takes about 60 seconds. That was a real life saver for us. It increased the quality of our dolls because we no longer had these globs of glue all over the eyes and they went on quicker and easier."

◆ ◆ ◆

__Nancy Walters__: "I began direct-sculpting in porcelain clay a year or so before I began making dolls. It seemed reasonable that I should use this method for dolls too. By the time I had heard that it couldn't be done, I had managed to master it with fair success. At that time I only knew of a couple of people who were doing one-of-a-kind dolls in porcelain clay, and I don't know of too many more who are doing it with any regularity now. Most people who do porcelain one-of-a-kinds resculpt from slipcast parts, which has a number of advantages, not the least of which is weight. The clay parts must be hollowed for firing, but it isn't possible to hollow them as thin as slip can be poured, so the resulting doll is heavier. The surface will never be as smooth as cast porcelain, which is fine - even preferable - for the kind of dolls I do but is less satisfactory for pretty dolls. And working in the clay takes longer since you must start from scratch each time. Despite the disadvantages, I like the immediacy and directness of the process; the clay is significantly more plastic than clays made by drying out commercial doll slip.

"Although I sculpt very haphazardly, undoubtedly forming countless air pockets as I work, I have learned to minimize the size of the pockets in problem areas around the eyes, etc. Through a system of venting and very slow and careful firing, most pieces survive their trips through the kiln without the cracking I encountered in the beginning. I was never happy with the blush china paint coat on the relatively rough clay, but I have found some stains that can be mixed into the clay body, which will survive the cone nine firing required to completely mature the porcelain clay I use. Although I have used and continue to use some of the polymer and cellulose clays, I continue to go back to the porcelain for about half my dolls.

"I have also been an enthusiastic user of paperclay since it became readily available several years ago. I was and still am skeptical about the strength of large pieces, so I make "bones" out of a stronger material and "skin" them with paperclay. Originally, I used Celluclay cores for legs and arms but now that Premier is available to provide strength without mixing, I use that unless the dolls are over about twenty inches."

◆ ◆ ◆

Maggie Iacono: "My special system is my house husband who takes care of all the cooking and cleaning. He knows where everything goes and what to touch and what not to touch. It really works out very well."

♦ ♦ ♦

Cindy McClure: "I believe that we all develop our own methods and that there isn't really a right or wrong way to do anything as long as it works for you. I am very open about the "how-tos" of my business."

♦ ♦ ♦

Ruth Treffeisen: "In working with porcelain, I follow traditional methods which have been proven over centuries. But I have found my own way of doing things with the bodies. The difficulty and complexity of developing a cloth body is very often underestimated. To create those patterns and not just to buy them is very demanding work."

♦ ♦ ♦

Fritz Wolff: "The best system is for Gretchen and I is to do our wet sculpting and designing here in Lexington, Kentucky. Then we take the design to our factory overseas and show the staff exactly how the piece is to be produced. They then produce the dolls according to our specifications. Each limited edition doll is then sent back to us so that Gretchen and I inspect every single one before signing it. This is a plus for collectors because we are able to hold down the cost of producing fine porcelain original dolls. Now, you don't have to be a doctor's wife to collect them."

♦ ♦ ♦

Jerri McCloud: "I think the thing that has kept us in business so long is that we really try to stay in touch with what the collectors want and not just what we like best or what seems to be the latest fad at the time. We are constantly in touch with the stores. We talk to people at all the shows and our annual convention. We send out periodic surveys and really listen to the feedback.

"Despite what comes and goes, we've found that collectors want realism - dolls that look like their neighbor's child, a niece or nephew, a grandchild, or some other little face they can relate to. They want dolls that evoke special memories for them and that's just what we try to produce. We must do a pretty good job or we wouldn't have been around this long."

Chapter Seven

PRODUCTION GOALS &
MARKETING STRATEGIES

It's not easy to convince people that you produce what they want to buy. Yet, each of today's top doll artists has successfully met this challenge. As the industry continues its upward surge and a constant stream of product floods the marketplace, doll artists face an unprecedented level of world-wide competition for the collector's attention. This means that somehow, amid a deluge of dolls, they must stand out and be noticed by the customers. Fortunately, artistic thinking takes root in creativity and that's where our top artists really dig in. Applying this creativity to production and marketing strategies assures the artist success and unearths some very interesting stories. Of course producing the best possible product keeps them in the game.

HOW DO YOU SET PRODUCTION GOALS & MARKETING STRATEGIES?

**Jan McLean**: "When I first started, dollmaking was just in its infancy and doll collecting was almost unheard of here in New Zealand. I taught from 1984 to 1991 and organized conventions to bring the world of dolls to New Zealanders. The conventions were very successful with many guests coming from the States to teach sculpting, painting, doll collecting, etcetera. Slowly, over the past six years, doll collecting has become more popular, especially now that the big companies like Franklin Mint and Hamilton have opened offices here. I've also helped to bring about an awareness of dolls by doing articles for many magazines, as an artist and a successful business woman. I was also featured in a national television program made to inspire others to be successful. I have talked to many different organizations and I tour many interested groups around the studio. I believe that all this has helped to bring dolls to "Down Under" and helped create a new market. It is an exciting time.

"I travel a great deal to Europe and the States to promote my work. For example, in 1995, I will be in a different country each month. For me it means being in the air for twenty-four hours to go to Germany. To go to New York it is eighteen hours in the air. I cross datelines and arrive at the same time I left. Strange feeling. I have to pinch myself to believe it is really happening. This type of traveling is very tiring but essential to keep a high profile. We now employ marketing consultants as the business has exploded, so we are constantly setting new goals."

◆ ◆ ◆

Rotraut Schrott: "I do one-of-a-kinds and want to present these dolls in good galleries, exhibitions, and museums. Since 1988, I have worked together with *The Great American Doll Company* (GADCO) to help accomplish my goals. They reproduce some of my designs in vinyl and porcelain for the American and European market with love and sensitivity. I also promote my dolls through my book, *Making Original and Portrait Dolls in Cernit*. This is available in English translation to the American market."

◆ ◆ ◆

Fritz Wolff: "Ten years ago the public wanted inexpensive porcelain dolls, but as more people got into the collector business, their tastes became more sophisticated and prices skyrocketed. We thought that there was a window of opportunity in today's market place for an artist series that's above the general market but below the super high priced collector dolls. We introduced a line of bone porcelain designer dolls at prices people could afford. That was our main goal. We produce 30 new sculptures each year."

◆ ◆ ◆

Hildegard Gunzel: "The challenge with working limited edition lines is that you must think ahead for the whole line. You have to plan years in advance for hair color, eyes, arms, legs and mechanics, to make sure that each year the collectors have something new to collect. Then when you have all that planned, you must think about materials, colors and textures.

"As for marketing strategies, I attend all the important fairs, place full-page adds in the doll magazines, publish my own books, and serve as a guest speaker or give demonstrations at the big doll conventions. That also offers me a chance for a closer contact with the buyers."

◆ ◆ ◆

__Maggie Iacono__: "We have a general idea of where we're heading and we discuss this regularly. Each morning over coffee we discuss that day's goals. It's important for us to keep communicating these things, to keep production running smoothly. As far as a marketing strategy goes, I let *European Artist Dolls* distribute my dolls. It's the best move I could have made. The whole business end of dollmaking, dealing with the stores and things like that, was disturbing to me and interrupted my work a lot. It's really nice to let them handle all of that. They also do all of the advertising so I don't have to deal with that either. I'm not a sales person by any means. I just make dolls."

◆ ◆ ◆

__Pat Secrist__: "It's kind of intuition with me. I get a feeling about how something should be. Some of my local peers tell me that I have tremendous natural instincts regarding the right thing to do in the market place. You have to understand the people, how they feel and what they want. Then you develop a plan to meet those needs. If you can do that, you're going to be very successful."

◆ ◆ ◆

__Cindy McClure__: "I have always set goals for myself. I think we all work better when we have deadlines. I set my goals so high that I really have to stretch to reach them, but I always manage to."

◆ ◆ ◆

Jerri McCloud: "Our marketing strategies are for the most part developed from our conversations with store owners and collectors. They tell us what they need and within our resources and capabilities, we try to fill that need. Ours is a consumer driven product. We have a wonderful collector society which meets once a year. At our annual convention we not only listen to what they think is good about our dolls, but also how they think we might improve them. Our production goals are based on how many dolls our work force can produce according to our standards. We do all of our own production and needless to say, we can only produce so much. Due to the training time involved with new employees, we cannot increase production over night."

◆ ◆ ◆

Paul Crees: "The art doll market is intense and competitive. One must go out there and grow with the public. To do this we travel with our work constantly. About three months of the year we are on the road. We advertise, produce brochures, newsletters and recently we have filmed a video. All these things must work together."

◆ ◆ ◆

Wendy Lawton: "I am no longer directly involved in setting goals and planning production. My partner, Linda Smith, handles this whole area of responsibility. It takes a tremendous amount of organization, from purchasing all the way to production management, to make certain that the schedule is met. The marketing of our dolls is accomplished according to an allotment system set up for our dealers several years ago."

◆ ◆ ◆

Ruth Treffeisen: "My dollmaking is always oriented on long term goals. My objective is not the fast sale of a few dolls, but rather to work together on a long-term basis with the lovers and collectors of Treffeisen dolls. I want to be able to stand up to the critical questions of the collectors. That is my very important goal."

◆ ◆ ◆

Uta Brauser: "My ethnic dolls sell absolutely across the board, not just to Blacks or Whites. So I do broad base marketing. I show my dolls in as many shows as I can and I advertise in all the major doll magazines as well as other publications (gift and art magazines when I have the money). I also do some signings in the stores.

"As far as production goals, I certainly do have to work within my available means, which is one nice limit. But I am also guided by passion and sometimes forget to consider the cost of producing certain things. However, I do make sure to cover the main successful lines first because they stand for my "daily bread." After that I can spend time and money on the crazy ideas and not care if they sell or not.

"One thing which I want very much to do is to help educate the Black community on dolls and doll collecting in general because Blacks in America seem to have little knowledge about dolls and sculpting. I want to help expose this community to the art form through maybe holding neighborhood workshops, because they have nothing like that happening here."

◆ ◆ ◆

Sherry Stephens: "I like to use pinking scissors. I like that little zig-zag seam inside. It makes it look so homemade. But nobody does that anymore; they all use their sergers. That bothers me a lot because I think it makes the dolls look so industrial. The problem is nobody wants to touch the stuff for a decent price without finished seams on a serger. As a goal, I have to let myself get in touch with the present and stop thinking in terms of pinking scissors.

"*Doll Makers International* handles my marketing for me, but on my own I'm still trying to get more people to get to know my dolls through the major doll shows, shop signings and the *Home Shopping Network*."

◆ ◆ ◆

Susan Wakeen: "Production is based on the number of incoming sales. Fortunately my husband sets the marketing goals based on our previous sales and future expectations based on current market conditions."

◆ ◆ ◆

Floyd Bell: "I work as a teacher and hope to be able to continue that for a long time. I really enjoy dollmaking, but I try to keep that as my hobby. I promote my work through the doll magazines and through the doll shows."

◆ ◆ ◆

Julie Good-Kruger: "I do long-range and short-range planning and goal-setting for myself. Production goals are based upon a number of factors, not the least of which involves how many employees we want (how big we want our business to be), how much production space we have, what kind of growth is actually healthy for the company, what the previous dealer base was, how many shows we feel like spending our time doing and so forth. These are personal decisions that my husband and I must make from year to year."

♦ ♦ ♦

__Patricia Rose__: "For me it's like instinct. After a few years of doing it, I just know how many dolls I can realistically produce and sell each year. Along with all the other responsibilities, that limit is about 125 dolls."

♦ ♦ ♦

__Janet Ness__: "I figure out how many dolls I can produce each month, allowing for enough time to do the trouble shooting, which can take up to 85% of an artists time, and enough time to do a very good job on the dolls. It's like running a marathon really. You've got to figure out your pace and what you can realistically get done. Then you have to stick with it.

"As far as marketing goes, I've got to plan out the advertising well in advance so that I can figure that expense into the wholesale price of the doll. It can cost as much as $3,000 for just one good ad, but it is worth it. The collector's like to see your name out there to feel that you are a stable artist and that you're not going to be here one year and gone the next. They need to see that I'm still actively producing dolls."

♦ ♦ ♦

__FayZah Spanos__: "Every year I set production and marketing goals, but I'm very realistic about them. I never set goals that are unattainable. The ones I do set, I strive with all my heart to keep. The marketing I do myself. It's all guess work but I have to trust my instincts and they're usually pretty good. Listening to what the collectors say helps too. They tell you what they want and expect. I base a lot on that."

◆ ◆ ◆

<u>*Nancy Walters*</u>: "My goals are more related to my own plea-
sure than they are to marketing at this time. I had vowed not
to get caught up in the commercial approach and to never
repeat a doll. Well, every artist has dolls that come along
from time to time that are really special. I had one of those.
It attracted a lot of attention. The next thing I knew, I had let
myself be talked into doing that same doll again. Although I
didn't try to do the identical doll and purposely made small
inconsequential changes, it wasn't a very interesting task. And
the finished doll didn't have the feel of the first one. So I
decided to do a similar doll in feel only and see how that
worked; number three was not bad and was purchased right
away. Figuring I was on a roll, commercially, I tried a fourth
version; before I finished the sculpture I realized I wasn't
having any fun at all, that I had said all I had to say on the
subject two dolls back. The result was an uninspired doll that,
while appealing to collectors, was a big disappointment to
me. The experience reminded me that commercial pressure
could cause me to take a wonderful occupation and turn it
into pure drudgery. I no longer attempt to make dolls con-
form to my ideas of what will sell best. That approach takes
the life out of my dolls and would undoubtedly lead to a long
line of adequate dolls, without a wonderful one among them.

"I do set goals for the number of dolls I want to complete
for a given show. Those goals are usually unrealistic, but even
if they are achievable, something inevitably causes me to fall
a little short. Still, I wind up with more work than if I didn't
hope to have so many, and I try not to beat myself up for the
shortfall.

"Fortunately, I am a "kept woman" and my doll income is not

85

not necessary to pay the mortgage or grocery bill. I honestly think that if I needed the income to survive, I would return to teaching rather than take the pleasant activity of dollmaking and make it a chore. However, I consider myself a professional and my primary goal is to create consistently good dolls in an artistic sense. I want those who collect them to feel emotionally involved with the piece and be happy to own them. If what I want to make isn't immediately a hit with a collector that's worrisome, but more acceptable to me than making dolls that bore me but sell."

♦ ♦ ♦

Karen Blandford: "My parents help me with the dollmaking. We generally aim at finishing one doll a week. I know that doesn't sound like a lot, but with all the disasters that can happen, this is sometimes not even possible. If any shop is in a hurry, we will always do our best to have something done by a certain deadline. Otherwise, we find that it's best to take our time and concentrate on doing everything right so we can be proud of it. This is very important to us.

"We feel that the best way to market our dolls is at the shows. There is so much that isn't seen in an advertisement. You can also get valuable feedback at the shows. Even people that would never purchase a doll have valuable comments."

♦ ♦ ♦

Wee Paulson: "After 35 years of dollmaking, I no longer have any marketing plans. I'm supposed to be retired. I'm not rich by any means, but if I can't sell a piece, I can at least enjoy giving it away.

"I have no goals either. I live one day at a time. When I get up in the morning and I'm still breathing and I feel pretty good, I'm just grateful to be alive. I'm glad that I've finally learned to enjoy the moment and to make things that bring joy to others."

◆ ◆ ◆

__Julia Rueger__: "This is not just a hobby for me. It's what I do to support myself, so I always have to think realistically about marketing my dolls. I can't afford to make a mistake. Today, unless you make something that's pretty and cutesy, it isn't going to sell as well and that's the real bottom line.

"I don't let anyone see a doll until it's all completed. Then I unveil it to Fritz (my manager), and a small circle of friends and neighbors to conduct an informal survey. This allows me to see what is liked and what isn't. Then I can make what changes I feel are necessary to complete the doll. I try to get people of different ages and backgrounds to give an opinion and sort of glean from that. When it's just right, I start advertising. We also offer a small rebate to stores who advertise our dolls and do a lot of co-op advertising."

◆ ◆ ◆

__Kathy Barry-Hippensteel__: "I love working for *Ashton Drake* because all I really have to do is design and sculpt, and that's what I'm good at. I'm not good at ordering wigs and eyes, and getting production done. I don't have time nor am I organized enough to do something like that. So I let them worry about it. They also do all the promoting of the dolls. I just show up at the signings and doll shows to meet with the collectors, which I really love doing anyway. I do hope to gradually get back into originals and some edition dolls of a larger size in the future."

◆ ◆ ◆

Marilyn Bolden: "When I first decided to make dolls as my business, I had no idea how many dolls I could do in a week or a month. Since my favorite part of dollmaking is designing and sculpting the models, I really like to have at least four new designs a year. At first I set my editions at 100 each, thinking that this would be a good number. I never thought about the fact that this meant 400 dolls to make. Since I can do only about 250 dolls a year, I soon realized that this wouldn't work. Now I'm doing editions of 30 to 50 and it's working out much better. Actually, just about every goal or strategy you come up with is a result of trial and error. You listen and learn from everyone in the business. Eventually you come up with a system that works for you.

"I sell my dolls through advertising in the doll magazines and by doing either *IDEX* or *Toy Fair* every year. I've tried several kinds of ads and eliminated those that were too expensive for the return they brought. Basically, my production goals are set by what I am physically capable of producing each year. My marketing strategies come from listening to collectors and shop owners and trying to come up with fresh new ideas for dolls that people will want to buy and that I love doing."

Chapter Eight

DISASTERS & BLOOPERS

Few things in life match the perfection of an exquisitely sculpted, beautifully painted, elaborately costumed art doll. Results like these, however, require tremendous effort on the part of the artists, who often sustain overwhelming setbacks in producing them. Despite many major disasters and minor bloopers, today's top doll artists amazingly persevere. In this chapter they openly share with us their worst dollmaking disasters ranging from the hilarious to the heartbreaking, to the nearly unbelievable! For many of the artists, sharing these stories was not easy. Some of the wounds were still too fresh. But for the sake of art and the love of dolls they confessed their worst mistakes and most exasperating moments. By sharing with us their laughter and tears, they offer us a perspective rarely seen in the doll world, and a deeper appreciation of the complex art of dollmaking.

WHAT WAS YOUR WORST DOLL-MAKING DISASTER OR BLOOPER?

Cindy McClure: "Even after investing several thousands of dollars to start my dollmaking business, it took a year and a half before I finally had a successful show. After such a struggle I had finally come to this one show loaded up with boxes of beautiful dolls and to my great elation, sold virtually every one. I was saved, or so I thought. While I was packing up to leave, I was robbed. They took all that I had made in a matter of seconds. I went from an extreme "high" to a devastating "low." I remember the heavy, empty feeling driving home from that show with no dolls and no money, just a police report."

◆ ◆ ◆

Pat Secrist: "To do a life-like human being is one of the most difficult tasks a sculptor can ever handle, especially if it's a child. After I'd sculpted my first few, I noticed that the face was kind of flat. The reason for that, of course, was that I was working in one dimension, looking only at the front without rotating the sculpture. It's a common mistake that new sculptors make, but it left me with a whole series of these flat faced dolls that I called, 'Wall Marked Dolls' because it looks like they ran face first into a wall. It was and still is really embarrassing."

◆ ◆ ◆

Julia Rueger: "I've had a few disasters that made me cry, but the one that stands out the most is a funny one. I was dyeing costumes, a very elaborate and tedious process that took hours.

I had just completed six costumes and laid them out to dry in the sun on some clean, flat cardboard in the front parking lot. Sometime in the late afternoon, a UPS truck came. When I went out to check the costumes, I found they were covered with tire tracks and a pair of the pants were missing! I got in my car and frantically took off down the road searching for the pants that had gotten stuck in the tire treads, but couldn't find them. The next day, when I told the driver what had happened, he said that I could put in a claim. I just laughed, imagining myself trying to explain that I lost my pants because a UPS truck ran over them! "

♦ ♦ ♦

Jerri McCloud: "Our worst dollmaking blooper was probably Walt Dinsey's Cinderella and Prince Charming. These dolls were an immediate sell out, which was wonderful. But when the stores started to receive them, the comments were that she looked like Carol Burnett! Well, converting a one dimensional product to three dimensional is not the easiest thing. We did not know that we should have taken artistic license to make them much more pleasing.

"When the time came to produce Snow White and the Seven Dwarfs, we submitted four different heads for Snow White. Disney chose one of the four the first time around! The set was tremendously successful and the first porcelain set ever made."

♦ ♦ ♦

Sherry Stephens: "I learned everything in a strange order, and it caused some problems. I started sculpting and working on the molds before I knew how to handle the china paints and greenware. One time I fired a dozen perfectly painted little faces in a kiln that was too hot. When I opened it up was

91

I ever shocked. Instead of seeing my beautifully finished heads, these blank faces stared back at me. All the paint had completely burned off! It was just horrible. I had worked so hard on those pretty little faces. I had to start all over."

♦ ♦ ♦

Hildegard Gunzel: "Twenty years ago, when I first started making dolls, I forgot to put in a separating medium between the two parts and my doll disappeared in the mold."

♦ ♦ ♦

Maggie Iacono: "The worst disaster I ever had happened when I made my first resin mold for a particular sculpture and hadn't mixed it right, with the correct amount of hardener to resin. I put it into my oven to cure and went out for a while. When we got back home, there was this horrendous smell coming from the basement. The whole mold had just melted in the bottom of the oven. It was just the worst mess and it took quite a long time to get it all out of there."

♦ ♦ ♦

Nancy Walters: "Years ago I decided to try a limited edition _Father Christmas_. I had made a couple of molds before, once in college where I carefully did everything the instructor told me and again years later as a press mold for clay; so I pretty much knew the drill. The second mold was made using some of my fantastic shortcut ideas and it took nearly three years to get all the plaster cleaned up from under the kitchen cabinets! I figured to make this mold with mold boards instead of shoe boxes and follow the rules. Soon I was very bored with pouring, cleaning, painting and dressing little heads all alike. I had done five and the planned fifteen looked light years away. Then I got another really great idea. Since earthenware clay was cheaper than porcelain or Super Sculpey, which I was using for my originals, I'd get a bag of that for the sculpt.

"Because I am such a klutz, I high-fired the clay sculpture rather than making molds from leather hard clay and possibly damaging the model. Since porcelain vitrifies, it separates from the mold fairly easily. Earthenware remains porous after firing, so even three coats of mold soap that had worked fine before, wasn't enough to effect a release. My husband appeared with mallets and chisels, and after 90 minutes or so we had a floor full of head parts and mold parts. The molds didn't seem to be too badly damaged, so it looked like I could use them; I set them aside to dry. Some days later I decided to pour the molds. I set the first one on the counter and began pouring in the slip. And I kept pouring. The heads were pretty big, but surely they couldn't hold half a gallon. As I peered intently into the mold, hoping to see the slip level rise, I realized something cold was rising from my sandal-clad feet. I finally figured out that the molds were more badly damaged than I had thought, as well as where the half gallon of slip was - I was standing in it. I gave up and buried the remaining earthenware in the backyard because I couldn't figure out what else to do with it. I Probably lost about $8 on the clay, another $3 on slip; it's hard to put a dollar value on mental anguish - you always wonder if feeling stupid a lot shortens your life."

◆ ◆ ◆

__Julie Good-Kruger__: "We have made many bloopers in terms of costliness, time, money and morale. The worst for our morale was in the beginning when we finally had our first ten prototype heads fired and discovered something was wrong with our china-paint. It all rubbed off even after it was fired. The next ten heads had the eyes cut out wrong, so that we couldn't set the eyes in the heads. In each case, everything had to be tossed out and we had to start all over. Our costliest error was waiting too long, one year, to order our garments. We had to set our production schedule back farther into the spring while we waited."

♦ ♦ ♦

Wendy Lawton: "There isn't one big disaster, though every day has it's share of mini-disasters. When you work with a "temperamental" medium like porcelain, you learn to plan disaster-preparedness into the schedule!"

♦ ♦ ♦

Peter Coe: "We haven't actually had a sculpting blooper, but we do have a drawer full of dreadful discarded costumes that are deeply offensive to the human eye and all those of a nervous disposition. We keep these things as a constant reminder of our weak moments of dubious artistic merit."

♦ ♦ ♦

Rotraut Schrott: "It is really very hard for me to write something about a dollmaking disaster, because up to this point I have not had any. You see, for one-of-a-kind dolls, I have to spend so much time and care that at the end all has to be absolutely right."

♦ ♦ ♦

Karen Blandford: "The worst disasters have been in moldmaking, when the mold box falls apart and the plaster goes everywhere and onto everything, walls, floor, table, me!

94

Pouring greenware can have its problems too. I've dropped a one gallon jar of slip and had it go all over the place. Sometimes the bands holding a mold together will not be strong enough and the slip will ooze out the bottom and get all over everything. Of course, when I have a disaster like this, the dogs will come over to see what's up, and then I have to clean them as well!"

♦ ♦ ♦

**Susan Wakeen**: "Our worst disaster was that our first four hundred dolls sold at a loss!"

♦ ♦ ♦

**Kathy Barry-Hippensteel**: "I am my own worst critic about everything. Sometimes I open up the mold and think, yeck, where was my mind when I made this thing? But, that sort of experience keeps me striving to do better."

♦ ♦ ♦

**Jan McLean**: "We sent a beautiful doll to Japan one time, but she was not finished. Her head was stuffed with a sweat shirt, with the wig attached to the sweat shirt. My son didn't realize that the doll was unfinished and sold it to a tourist. So, somewhere is Japan is an unfinished Jan McLean doll!"

♦ ♦ ♦

**Patricia Rose**: "My blooper was a doll that I made in wax over porcelain! It's a mess!"

♦ ♦ ♦

Fritz Wolff: "I think a lot of times designers are ahead of the times, as far as what the general public wants, and they get a little too artistic. It might be a great design, but that doesn't mean that the public is going to respond to it. So I think that some of the designs that I've done over the years, that I've really personally liked a great deal, were maybe too expressive or had too much character. We're known in our line for having character dolls, but you can only take that so far. The general public wants more of a pretty doll. I tend to make mine look more like real people.

"Very few of us in the human race are good looking, according to Hollywood's standards. Most of us are just kind of ordinary. Some of us are too fat or too skinny with dimples in the wrong place, but that's okay. That's real. The problem is that people in the doll world don't want to face that reality. I'll give you an example. All three of my children had to go to the orthodontist. That's real life. So I sculpted a doll with buck teeth. I thought she was really cute, but nobody else liked her. Nobody else thought it was funny. She died on the shelf."

♦ ♦ ♦

Uta Brauser: "I really can't remember the worst blooper, since this profession is generally just full of disasters. Working with human beings, there is always that percentage of human failure or carelessness. Maybe I should just count how often I came close to a heart-attack!"

♦ ♦ ♦

Marilyn Bolden: "Every day seems to bring some new little goof. We are such a small operation that we don't have the luxury of being able to do a lot of extra parts. Invariably the head I need most will have a speck on the nose and have to be discarded or a leg or shoulder will crack when fired. More than once I've ended up with two left legs for a doll that had to go out the next day. But those things are really just minor annoyances that set back your schedule for a few days.

"I suppose the closest I've come to what could be called a disaster would be the problem I had recently with one of my new dolls. This doll proved really popular and I had a lot of orders for her. I had all my supplies in and was anxious to get started, but my mold maker hadn't finished the arm and leg molds. When he finally got them to me, I rushed to get the first dolls ready for shipment and sent them out without realizing that the groves in the mold where the arm attaches to the body was not deep enough. Customers who bought the first dolls were bending the arms and pulling them off. After getting several dolls returned for repair, I corrected the fault with the mold and have had no problem since. Anytime you ship dolls that have a defect like this it's quite embarrassing, but you just have to learn from your mistakes and go on."

◆ ◆ ◆

Floyd Bell: "I used polyester fabric on a historical doll, Scott Joplin. He lived in the 1920s and, as it was later pointed out to me, back then there was no such thing as polyester fabric. I was much more careful with my research after that experience."

◆ ◆ ◆

Ruth Treffeisen: "I am celebrating my tenth year as a dollmaker. Fortunately, a really big dollmaking disaster never happened to me."

◆ ◆ ◆

__Janet Ness__: "I had a delivery date to meet with Robyn, one of my first limited edition dolls, and went over to my new seamstress to pick up the fifty dresses she'd made. They were the worst nightmare I'd ever seen! There were holes cut in the fabric where she had snipped threads, they didn't fit the dolls, and all the finish work on them looked as if a child had done it. I had fifty dolls due and no costumes to put them in! All that expensive material was destroyed. I went home and just wept hysterically, certain I was ruined.

"When my husband saw the dresses, he realized my desperate situation and said, 'Janet, I'm going to take two weeks off from work and after you show me how, you and I will sew those costumes.' So, for two weeks he sat at the serger night and day sewing petticoats, bloomers, and aprons while I worked on the dresses. It was an unbelievable scramble, but they turned out beautifully and we were only a week late with the delivery of those dolls. But, what an awful experience!"

♦ ♦ ♦

__Wee Paulson__: "I make what people would call bloopers on purpose, because I don't like perfect! Most of my dolls are bowlegged. I wire them and pack the knees so they'll be a little knock need because mine are that way. Their hair is messed up and their smiles are a little crooked. If I make a slip, I simply turn it into another character trait. I'd rather have things be not too perfect and have more character. I also love materials that are soft and kind of washed out and worn looking, not crisp and new, because I portray real children and that's how real kids look. Slightly less than perfect is exactly the look I want."

♦ ♦ ♦

**FayZah Spanos**: "I was out of the country when a shipment of over 1,000 dolls went out to the *Home Shopping Network*. To my horror, I discovered that every one of those dolls went out without a signature. Every one of them! And they were scheduled to go on the air in two days! I had to take a crew with me and fly to three different warehouses, in three different states and open every shipper, every gift box, and untie every doll from the inserts. Then I had to sign each one and tie them back in and redo all of the packaging of over one thousand dolls. That was a major boo-boo."

FayZah Spanos

Chapter Nine

GREAT DISCOVERIES & PROJECTS

The history of dollmaking is filled with trail blazing pioneers who established the art, developed time-proven mediums, and laid the foundation upon which the standards of dollmaking will forever be built. In that same tradition many of today's top dollmakers continue to carve out new paths for future dollmakers to follow. This chapter demonstrates how these artists use their creative talents to expand and improve upon the techniques of the past, find new methods of operation, modernize equipment, interchange components, develop new mediums, make use of computer technology, and adapt to an ever-changing market. Many of the discoveries divulged in this chapter sit on the cutting edge of today's dollmaking technology and will become a part of tomorrow's dollmaking history.

101

WHAT WAS YOUR GREATEST DOLLMAKING DISCOVERY OR PROJECT?

Paul Crees: "We choose wax because there is a softness to the look and feel of it that you simply can't get with any other medium, although wax can be an especially difficult medium in which to work. We developed a specially formulated wax with various polymers and resins added for extra strength. This formula absorbs shock, making the dolls almost unbreakable. We also designed detachable arms that allow for quick snap-in replacement, should breakage occur.

"Another technical achievement we've developed is a two-tone wax process which is done while the wax is still hot. The effect is dramatic. Though the process is difficult, we feel we owe it to the collectors to be diversified in our artistic output. We do like to think we are constantly stretching the boundaries."

♦ ♦ ♦

Marilyn Bolden: "When I first decided to sell my dolls I was probably the most naive person in the business. While I had been an artist for years and thought I was a pretty good sculptor, I knew only the basics about working in porcelain and practically nothing about marketing dolls. But I jumped right in and took my first dolls to the _New York International Toy Fair_, in New York City. This experience could have been devastating but I watched what was going on and I listened to what everyone was saying and I learned. What I learned there was the my greatest discovery. Basically, what it boils down to is that it doesn't matter how great you think your dolls are. If they aren't the type of dolls collectors are buying, the stores won't stock them and you may be out of business soon. You have to know what is selling and adjust your product accordingly."

◆ ◆ ◆

Janet Ness: "I worked very hard to develop a finish for the doll's heads that makes them sort of iridescent and gives them a lot more life. The feedback from it so far has been great. It is my own special formula and it gives my dolls the luminous look of the antiques. Of course it's a secret."

◆ ◆ ◆

Floyd Bell: "Through extensive research in doll literature and surveys of the doll industry, I discovered that there were very few good Black historical dolls on the market and decided to change all that. When I finally learned to carve faces that actually looked like my subjects, that was great."

◆ ◆ ◆

Julia Rueger: "I did a special one-of-a-kind 30 inch African woman out of earthenware. She's unlike anything else I've ever done. She has the authentic pattern scaring carved into her face like some African women do. There is a decorative wire coming out of her bottom lip and her nose and ears are pierced. She also has wire coils wrapped around her neck and her hair is waxed. I made the costume out of authentic mudcloth, bought in Africa, and used actual African accessories. She's turned out great, but she is definately the most unusual doll I've ever done."

◆ ◆ ◆

103

Pat Secrist: "Most recently that would be our eyes. We're the only manufacturer of acrylic doll eyes in the United States. Our eyes are called *Real Eyes* because they are very life-like. We've had optometrists tell us that they've never seen anything better. We developed not only the eye, which took me several years, but we also invented all the equipment to make them.

"But my first great discovery was taking a porcelain doll and offering it in a vinyl medium. At that time, there was only one other company in the world doing it. I created my own version of a life-like porcelain vinyl that looked just like porcelain but cost half as much. That was a life changing experience for me."

◆ ◆ ◆

Nancy Walters: "I hate doll stands and feel that they detract considerably. My first system to eliminate this was rods extending from the legs of the dolls which fitted into holes in the base. Still not happy, I embedded copper tubes in the legs with removable tempered steel wire (piano wire) pins to connect the two. At the time I "discovered" this, I didn't know anyone else who was doing it. I passed the method on to several other doll artists, including a friend who had been attaching his dolls to the bases. He began to use the technique, with some variation, and described it in his first dollmaking book. Over time, I noticed that more and more people were using the copper tube method. Some may have developed it themselves, but most probably they learned it via the doll artist grapevine from my discovery.

"I also came up with a hat anchoring system, after chasing several large-brimmed hats that wafted from heads and sailed off to the lakes around which so many Florida outdoor shows are held. Making marionettes to sell at a lower cost than dolls was sometimes a necessity in order to make a profit at some of the art shows. I used to slice off the tops or backs of the heads to hollow out the porcelain, then replace the piece. Then I began replacing the clay "pates" with slices of foam balls. They could be sliced and shaped to fit any head and cut down considerably on weight. Then I drove large hat pins straight into the "brains" of those ladies. It worked great.

"Most of my dolls have been on cloth bodies with wire armatures. A hard-stuffed muslin body works fine under most types of costuming, but there were times when I wanted pot bellies or other subtle sags and bags that I couldn't achieve with muslin appliques. I stitched on sections of knit fabrics, usually pieces of old tights, padded them as desired, and tacked the skin and padding into place. During these experiments I was in touch almost daily with Bob McKinley, (recently deceased) who began playing around with the same process; he was the first one of us to "skin" the entire body. So many of the procedures I have used came from ideas we bounced off each other and experiments we engaged in simultaneously. Fortunately, he left many of these techniques for future artists in his books and tapes."

◆ ◆ ◆

Patricia Rose: "I designed a series of lady dolls which are totally unique to the industry. They are 18 inches tall, all porcelain, anatomically correct, have movable arms and legs and can wear sensual dresses with the shoulders bare, while showing no body joints."

◆ ◆ ◆

Sherry Stephens: "I made up my own two layered body design using both muslin and polyester material. Many doll bodies are

105

made of muslin only, but muslin rots as it ages and the body falls apart. Polyester has a great feel to it, but it's too stretchy. So what I did was make my bodies out of two layers of "skin." The inner body is muslin with a polyester skin over that. The muslin keeps the polyester from stretching out and the polyester gives the doll a nice feeling. Plus polyester will not rot. It'll lay in a land fill forever."

♦ ♦ ♦

Cindy McClure: "I don't mean to tease, but my greatest idea and discovery is about to be born. I just can't tell you what it is at this time."

♦ ♦ ♦

Uta Brauser: "You see, what I do is sculpt people and feelings, so I can sculpt a baby or I can sculpt an old man or a lovely woman. I have no limits to my work and no fears of doing anything.

"My Black contemporary dolls are very popular but they are as political as their subjects. Today's Black youth are proud of who they are and that comes through in my dolls. You see, certain things are very Black and are not part of what is being integrated into mainstream. I am able to reproduce these distinct characteristics in my dolls. That is why a lot of Black people comment to me that I really capture their character. I think also that they are surprised at this because they don't expect a white person to see and understand these things."

♦ ♦ ♦

Wee Paulson: "I don't use patterns. I just kind of cut and think muscle as I go. Rather than using traditional fiber fills to stuff my

106

dolls, I use surgical cotton because fiber fills are too soft. Surgical cotton can be packed harder to give more muscle definition and allows each of my felt characters to stand on it's own. And I've recently started making the eyes out of clay rather than painting them on. Then I glue them in place and sculpt an eyelid to encase them. This gives them much more form than they used to have."

◆ ◆ ◆

Hildegard Gunzel: "Every new idea is always the greatest, until another new one comes along."

◆ ◆ ◆

Wendy Lawton: "The discoveries are never earth-shaking. It's just one tiny idea after another. The real gratification comes when you can capture the imagination of the collector. Dollmaking is less about discoveries and more about reaching out to people."

◆ ◆ ◆

Fritz Wolff: "That would be our life-sized, weighted baby Berkeley, made in the Danish tradition of having two bodies. The inner body is filled with crushed granite. Then there is an inch of cotton batting between the inner and outer muslin body. It feels like a soft body and weighs about eight pounds.

"We also recently brought back a line of *Pocket Dolls* with 100% porcelain heads, arms, bodies and legs, as they were once produced in the 1860s in Germany. We recreated the 12 inch *Pocket Dolls* using our most famous original designer heads."

◆ ◆ ◆

__Maggie Iacono__: "People tell me that the thing which stands out most about my work is that I've come out with the smoothest face possible in felt. This surface fools the eye so that many people looking straight at my dolls have to touch them to know if they are porcelain or felt.

"I've also come up with a ball jointed body, which I don't think anyone else has ever done in cloth. It's an eleven piece jointed body, which allows the dolls to be very poseable instead of just standing there. Collectors tell me that, as a result of this, now they're playing with my dolls and I think that's great."

◆ ◆ ◆

__Karen Blandford__: "The best thing I ever discovered was the armature we use for the dolls. It gives you the ability to do just about anything, pose-wise. Also, learning how to use the white porcelain was a big step forward. The extra work is really worthwhile for the finished look."

◆ ◆ ◆

__Rotraut Schrott__: "To sculpt portrait dolls after a living model is very difficult. This is the biggest challenge for me but I have learned to sculpt the dolls in a way that reflects the personality of the child. To do that, I have to completely clear my mind and leave behind my own ideas. I must concentrate only on the child.

"I think my greatest project was a pretty little girl named Nicole. Her mother wanted to surprise her grandmother at Christmas with a life-sized portrait doll of her. It was a happy time sculpting her and Nicole, the doll, was ready by Christmas. On Christmas Eve the whole family assembled in their living-room waiting for the grandmother to arrive. Nicole, the doll, was sitting in a comfortable chair. When the grandmother walked in, she went straight up to my portrait and said, 'Hello, Nicole.' After a short moment she realized that it was a doll and not her real granddaughter! As an artist, I was very excited and gratified to hear that story."

◆ ◆ ◆

FayZah Spanos: "I don't think I've done anything special that's never been done before. My work is just a combination of a lot of good techniques, plus my own ideas about what makes a beautiful baby. I've tried many different things, like an all porcelain tushy, on my doll called *Angel Cheeks*. She had a little peek-a-boo seat with ruffles in the back, that exposed the cutest little bottom. Some people thought it was adorable, some people thought it was inappropriate. I've tried little chest plates on my babies and that seemed to work well.

"Another thing I've found that people enjoy about my dolls is that they have soft cloth bodies packed with pellets and poly fill to give them the weight and make them more cuddly. They are very hard to resist, even for me. Once you pick them up, you don't want to put them down. I've been known to walk around the shop with these babies straddled on my hips just because they are so fun to hold and cuddle."

◆ ◆ ◆

Julie Good-Kruger: "We have always done our very best every step of the way. Our first dolls had a complicated body system of wood and wire inside, making the arms poseable. A copper tube went inside the torso, enabling the doll to stand up on a wood base with a dowel going into the body. This way I avoided the wire around the waist of the normal doll stand. We experimented with composition doll bodies, and even an expandable foam, covered with stretch fabric. Today, we do mostly vinyl editions, but all our dolls are stand-up children."

◆ ◆ ◆

Jan McLean: "At this very moment we are just developing a new method for cleaning greenware. We are thrilled that we have managed to eliminate a lot of problems with it. We are still in the early stages, so we can't get more specific than that until it is perfected, but we are very excited about it."

◆ ◆ ◆

Susan Wakeen: "I haven't discovered anything that I am aware of. Honestly, my biggest surprise is that I can actually make dolls that people want to buy. It still surprises me and I love the challenge of it all. I have a great sense of personal satisfaction when I read the kind letters I receive from people who tell me of the pleasure they have felt from one of my dolls."

◆ ◆ ◆

Jerri McCloud: "For many years my goal was to make dolls look like real children instead of the "doll look" of the years prior. With Emily, in 1984, we succeeded. Now almost all dolls look like someone's child, grandchild, or neighbor. This was a major change for the doll industry."

◆ ◆ ◆

Kathy Barry-Hippensteel: "*Ashton Drake* and *Literacy Volunteers of America*, whose spokesperson was Barbara Bush, joined forces in an effort to promote literacy. They asked me come up with a doll for the project so I designed *Alex*, a little boy reading a book. I got to fly to Washington to personally present the doll to Barbara Bush. Famous people don't impress me but when President Bush walk in, my jaw dropped to the ground. He was coming around to shake hands and there I stood with the doll in one hand and the book in the other with no place to set the stuff down. I was so frustrated because after all that, I never did get to shake his hand. But being there was awesome and I got to give Barbara Bush a personally signed *Tickles*.

"I don't know what my greatest discovery is because I think it's out there there waiting for me to find it. But, I'm afraid that if I find it, I won't want to sculpt anymore because I will have achieved perfection. So, it's okay with me that I'm just dabbling along, and if I never really find perfection that's okay too because I've enjoy the search so much."

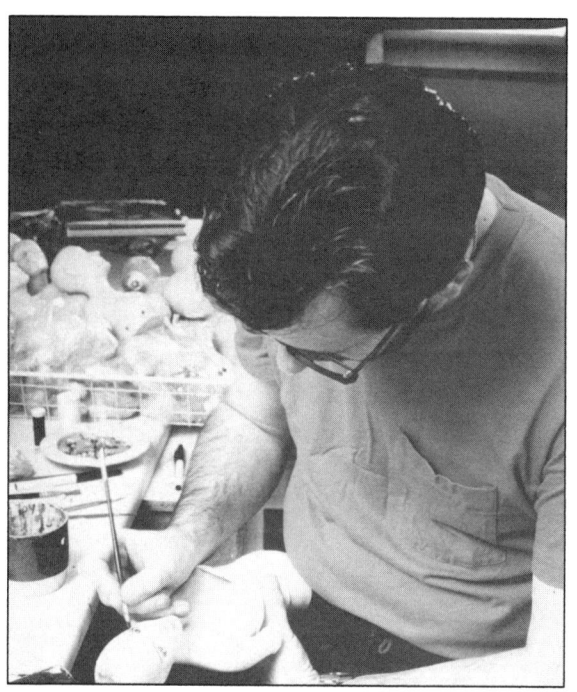

Paul Crees

Chapter Ten

ADVICE TO COLLECTORS

With the ever increasing complexity of today's doll market, it is very easy for collectors to become entangled in a sticky web of uncertainty. Should they buy the doll they love or the one that's sure to increase in value? Should they go for antiques or contemporary dolls? How can they tell if a piece is authentic or a pirated copy? The list of questions and choices is staggering and mistakes costly. Doll artists can help by offering us valuable insight into the art of collecting. They can advise us on potential problem areas which may never have occurred to us before. Through their candid, unbiased comments, we gain straight forward "insider" advice about doll collecting, from the people who know the most.

113

WHAT ADVICE CAN YOU OFFER DOLL COLLECTORS?

Janet Ness: "My advice to collectors is to become more educated about dolls. Learn more about things like the quality and durability of the costuming, the difference between plastic and glass eyes, body construction, wigs, and the different mediums. This knowledge will help make sure that you are getting the very best doll for your money. And don't be afraid to go back to the shop or the artist and tell them about any flaws you may have discovered after you purchased the doll, like a pit in the porcelain, a crooked eye, or a bad seam in the costume.

"Also, collectors should be aware that they need to plan ahead and budget their doll allowance. I see so often where people start buying the real low end dolls until they end up with a lot of them. Then they don't have a chance or the ability to buy some of the nicer quality pieces that do go up more in value."

♦ ♦ ♦

Peter Coe: "Collectors should buy what they enjoy, what they see as beautiful, amusing and evocative. Never buy for short-term investment. Appreciate the "classic" mediums of porcelain and wax and wood. These are proven to be durable mediums. Be aware that most modern materials used now in dollmaking are quite new and have not stood the test of time.

"Collectors should also learn to understand the industry

114

meaning of the words original, limited edition, and one-of-a-kind. Much confusion is caused by misunderstanding these terms. If an expensive doll is labeled original, always ask, 'how original.' Ask if the mold was hand made by the artist. Is the body soft or sculpted? Ask who sculpted the head, arms and legs. If the doll's parts look like every other doll you have seen then be suspicious. It may mean that most of the doll has been put together using commercial molds. If the doll is a one-of-a-kind, ask if the mold or original has been either destroyed or certainly not used again for any purposes. Always ask if the sculpture is a direct sculpt into the material used or was the material pressed into a mold to obtain a generic copy and then re-worked.

"Price is the most confusing point of all. Many new artists enter the market at very high prices matching and sometimes even exceeding those of more established artists. High prices like these should be avoided, particularly if the artist's name is new. In general, the doll collector really must be more discerning and much more questioning and demanding, particularly with today's high prices because the most important thing is to be really happy and quite satisfied with the quality, originality and durability of the piece you have purchased."

◆ ◆ ◆

Patricia Rose: "I feel very strongly that collectors should buy as many books as they can, to learn as much about dolls as they can."

◆ ◆ ◆

Floyd Bell: "At first I was hesitant about collecting dolls. I was concerned about what others would think about a man who buys dolls for himself. What a pity that was! I watched the dolls I liked get snapped up right and left. My advice is to go for it before they are gone. Great dolls, like great art, are just nice to have around you. They communicate in a special way and each one has it's own story to tell. Dolls have a mystical relationship with humans that I call doll magic."

◆ ◆ ◆

Karen Blandford: "Buy a doll because you just have to have it, not because it might be a good investment. Also, find out how much of the actual work was done by the artist themselves. This helps ensure the quality of the work.

"There are so many different styles and prices of dolls, and so many attitudes to what is a "real" doll for collectors and what isn't. Your collection should make you happy when you look at it, no matter how much the doll costs. In my collection I have dolls from *Ashton-Drake* to *Annette Himstedt* porcelain. I bought every one because I loved it. Of course the quality is important too, but you will usually find that dollmakers put so much into their work that they won't want to sell a doll unless it is of quality. After all, their name is on the doll."

◆ ◆ ◆

Nancy Walters: "Collectors need to educate themselves about what is out there and the reasons for varying prices. For true empathy, nothing beats making a doll; you will begin to understand the skill and time and costs involved. But most collectors don't really want to know that much. For them the best thing is to read the doll magazines and books like this one and talk to the artists. Find out the size of their editions and whether the whole doll is a new sculpt or only the head. Do they plan to issue the same doll in a different costume sometime? Are they going to sell a small edition of dolls and then sell the mold to the hobby dollmaking industry? If they do one-of-a-kinds, are all their dolls substantially different from one another or do most of the faces look pretty similar? You can't assume anything from the price; there are simple dolls in very large editions that sell for more than more detailed dolls in small editions by better known artists. There are editions of expensive dolls which sell out fast, while some less expensive dolls may sell only one or two. There are mediocre artists whose work sells quite well and highly regarded artists in the art world whose work doesn't sell well at all. You have to know what you are looking for - and looking at - and evaluate what it is worth to you.

"Some collectors have told me that they can't afford dolls that cost $1,000 or $2,000, yet they spend over that per year on less expensive dolls. Obviously, they can afford the more expensive dolls if they want to sacrifice quantity for quality. It has taken me 10 years to acquire 30 dolls at prices ranging from a rare low of $200 to a high of over $3,000. I would prefer to buy one doll a year or every other year, to get dolls that have great meaning to me, even though I might not be able to have every doll I want. Others would rather be able to buy nearly every doll that strikes their fancy. Collectors need to think this out, though, before saying they can't afford artist dolls."

◆ ◆ ◆

Ruth Treffeisen: "Doll lovers come from all levels of society and all age groups. They must have a feeling for beautiful things, and be able to see and appreciate the artistic expression in the doll and the style."

◆ ◆ ◆

FayZah Spanos: "Be aware of all the copies that are out there and all the reproductions that are being passed off as originals. That is a real problem because there are so many pirates that copy molds and sell dolls out of a truck or at flee markets for practically nothing. I've had collectors come into the showroom thinking that they bought an original of mine in porcelain and I see that it isn't. They have a right to get angry because someone lied to them! I feel very badly about this serious problem. That is why many artist won't sell to reproduction companies. I'm not sure I will much longer either. Today's collectors must be aware of this potential when making a purchase and be certain that they're getting the real thing, not just a copy."

◆ ◆ ◆

Uta Brauser: "I think the collectors must judge the quality of the piece which may not always go hand in hand with artistic expression. One has to clearly separate the two. Many times pieces have such incredible character and intensity but fall short of perfection in craftsmanship. Perhaps collectors should be aware of this a bit more and be more tolerant in some cases."

◆ ◆ ◆

Wee Paulson: "I don't generally give advice, but I do think collectors must consider what appeals to them and the amount of space available to them for the dolls. Many people collect all these dolls and have no where to put them so they just put them in boxes in closets or under beds. Why buy a doll if you can't see it? Dolls should be enjoyed and displayed. You should have room enough to do this."

◆ ◆ ◆

Pat Secrist: "The most important thing for a collector is to buy what you like - to buy what makes you feel good. Dolls are like flowers. When you give somebody a bouquet of beautiful flowers, what is the effect? It creates a pleasant feeling inside them that lasts until the flowers die. A doll should do the same thing for a collector. If it doesn't give you a pleasant emotional response then you have no business buying that doll. Do not buy a doll purely for investment value. Buy first because you love it, then if it goes up in value that's even better."

◆ ◆ ◆

Jerri McCloud: "Find out everything you can about the artist and the company that you have chosen. On more than one occasion when talking to collector's about a doll they purchased, I discovered that they did not know that the doll was produced overseas and yet this was important to them.

"Find out what the artist's involvement in production is, if any. There is a term call "tweaking" a mold. This means taking a commercial mold, laying clay into it, and changing it somewhat. There is no artistic challenge or creativity to this practice, just irresponsibility. Don't be afraid to ask the artist if he/she had help with the sculpting of that particular doll or whether it is totally original. An honest artist will not be insulted. It will just give him/her the chance to explain their sculpture. They will also be pleased with the fact that you are carefully investigating your potential investment. As a doll artist, of course I want you to collect my dolls, but it's more important to me to develop a good rapport with all collectors."

◆ ◆ ◆

119

Julia Rueger: "Collectors should always look at the quality of the work, from the costume to the painting, and find out all you can about the artist. How much of the work does the artist actually do? This should all be considered for the overall value of the doll. So, if you love the doll and are happy with the answers to all your questions, then you probably have a good investment."

◆ ◆ ◆

Maggie Iacono: "Go with what you love, what appeals to you. Don't worry about whether it will increase in value because there are no guarantees about which dolls will take off. Just look for quality and detail and go with what you love."

◆ ◆ ◆

Sherry Stephens: "The first thing a collector should do is start reading doll magazines to educate themselves so that they know about the different artists and learn what is original and what is reproduction. If you want dolls for an investment, you should start out with an artist's original doll that's not going to be reproduced by someone else. From those special dolls, pick one that you like. Going to the doll shows is a good idea too, because you will get to see a large number of dolls at one time and meet the artists."

◆ ◆ ◆

Hildegard Gunzel: "My advice to collectors is to only buy dolls from renowned doll artists. Make inquiries into their credentials before buying. Be sure of what you are getting because some dolls may be just copies."

◆ ◆ ◆

Susan Wakeen: "My first and foremost advice to collectors is to collect what you love. It is difficult at best to know which dolls will increase in value. Secondly, try to understand the value of what you are paying for. There are dolls made in the Orient, dolls made in the U.S. and dolls made in other countries. Many factors effect the price. Some dolls are open edition and some are limited edition. Some dolls have glass eyes, some have acrylic, some have human hair while others have synthetic, and some dolls are made with fine cottons, wools, or silks while others are made with less expensive polyesters and cottons."

◆ ◆ ◆

Julie Good-Kruger: "Many collectors are told that they should get this or that for investment potential or to round out their collection, or because something is rare. I really think what matters is what you truly like. For people who are just starting to collect, I would suggest not buying real expensive dolls at first, until your sensibility, or taste in dolls, is more developed. Your taste in dolls will change, especially at the beginning of collecting. I would suggest that you read the magazines, look at as many dolls as possible, join a *UFDC* club and learn about dolls. You will learn to appreciate some things that you did not notice before. It is also fun to spend time with other people who enjoy your hobby.

"I recommend that you set a budget for yourself, which disciplines your collecting and helps you narrow down your choices to what you really like and want the most. After you have been collecting for a while, you can re-evaluate which dolls have brought you the most pleasure, and rethink the price range you are in."

◆ ◆ ◆

**Cindy McClure**: "Collect whatever you can love and live with."

♦ ♦ ♦

**Jan McLean**: "My advice would be to buy the dolls that appeal to you, that you enjoy looking at. If they turn out to be a good investment, then that is a bonus."

♦ ♦ ♦

**Rotraut Schrott**: "The first and most important thing collectors should do, is train their eyes to recognize the "tweakers". These are so called doll artists who are thieves of the ideas or designs which belong to the real artists. The collector must buy carefully and be informed. If they prefer a quality one-of-a-kind, the price will be higher than that of a series doll. If the collector chooses series dolls, they should make sure that the anatomy is correct and compare prices. They should also study the painting on a doll. This is very important.

"On the other hand, the feeling for a particular doll varies from collector to collector. Perhaps a doll may not be perfect at all, but very lovable and the collector falls in love with it despite its faults. If they feel that way, they should act fast. Collecting is a passion and for such passion you should let your heart speak."

♦ ♦ ♦

**Kathy Barry-Hippensteel**: "Some lady walked by my booth at a show, not knowing I was behind her. She took one look at a doll I'd done and said, 'Oh, that one is so ugly. It looks just like a frog.' When I overheard that comment I was absolutely crushed! So, my advice to collectors is a little bit different. Never, never degrade a piece at a show, no matter how much you might dislike it, because you never know who's listening or whose feelings you

122

might hurt. Besides, what you see in a piece might be entirely different from what someone else sees in that same piece."

♦ ♦ ♦

Fritz Wolff: "I feel that as a collector, you should collect dolls because you like a certain artist or the look of a particular a doll. Then enjoy what you've purchased. Never buy something that you won't really enjoy, just because you heard it might go up in value. Those things are so subjective. Buy with your heart not your head and you'll never be disappointed."

♦ ♦ ♦

Marilyn Bolden: "My advice to collectors is to find a reputable shop that they like to deal with and stick with them. If a shop gets to know you as a regular customer, they will keep you advised of new dolls coming out on the market, provide you with pictures or catalogs and help you in making selections. Their assistance is invaluable in making sure you get the best doll for your money. Many stores are in personal contact with the artists and can get dolls signed for you or get certain issue numbers or find older dolls that you may be looking for."

♦ ♦ ♦

Wendy Lawton: "Because doll collecting is a very personal hobby, I like to suggest to collectors that they collect dolls they feel they simply cannot do without, dolls that make them feel happy, and dolls which they will feel comfortable displaying in their home. This is what I do, and I have a wonderful mixed collection of contemporary and antique dolls that I love."

♦ ♦ ♦

123

Sherry Stephens

Chapter Eleven

ADVICE TO DOLLMAKERS

The great artist, Michelangelo, was quoted as having said, "If people knew how hard I had to work to gain my mastery, it wouldn't seem wonderful at all." Those who have ever attempted the fine arts, understand the complexities involved in mastering the many difficult techniques, that lead one down the path of perfection. Passion is a merciless task-master that continually drives an individual beyond normal realms, to a higher plateau. So it is with today's top doll artists. For the love of dolls, they persevered and overcame the obstacles. For most, the struggle was long and difficult. However, these featured doll artists have made it to the top of their profession. In this final chapter, they offer their best advise for all those who would try their hand at dollmaking.

WHAT ADVICE CAN YOU OFFER ASPIRING DOLLMAKERS?

Patricia Rose: "Be positive! Work hard, keep trying, stay on top of your business and constantly come up with hot new ideas. Never sit on your last success too long. Keep it happening. Research, study, challenge yourself and question everything in the study of anatomy and structure. Shield yourself from all the ugly things in the world because if you want to create beautiful things, you must be beautiful inside. And with God's help you can become just that."

◆ ◆ ◆

Jan McLean: "The desire to make dolls is a wonderful disease. Though it consumes you, it is not fatal. If you are considering dollmaking classes, I caution you to carefully check the credentials and the work of any teachers you may be going to."

◆ ◆ ◆

Cindy McClure: "My advice to perspective dollmakers is to go for it! There is plenty of room for everyone who wants to be involved in the dollmaking industry and we're a great family to be a part of! Just keep at it every day and don't give up. I am always surprised that most beginners assume that all they have to do is take one seminar to be a professional. Sculpting is just like playing the piano . . . hats off to anyone who can sit down and play Mozart the first time, much less after a couple of years of lessons!"

◆ ◆ ◆

**Hildegard Gunzel**: "Practice making heads over and over again, and choose only the best to make into dolls. Be careful what you choose to do. Not every doll is worth making in porcelain."

◆ ◆ ◆

**Marilyn Bolden**: "My advice is for dollmakers who want to make dollmaking a full time business. First and foremost, you have to get your name known by collectors. Your goal is to have customers going into doll stores and asking for your dolls. This means you have to advertise regularly and hopefully get the stores to advertise your dolls too. Remember that most of your sales will be done by photographs. You must have great pictures of your dolls. Shop around for a photographer who works well with you. Just because someone is considered a good photographer doesn't mean he can take good doll pictures. The best doll photographers can capture your doll's personality so they seem to speak to collectors. Also, while you don't want to over price your dolls, remember that photos and advertising aren't cheap and you need to consider this when calculating the cost of making each doll."

◆ ◆ ◆

**Jerri McCloud**: "The business of dollmaking is tough. Are you sure this is really what you want to do? Recognize that the easy part is making the first doll and be fair with your collectors by producing the very best you can, each and every time. Also, familiarize yourself with doll collecting, artist proofs, prototypes and reproductions to thoroughly know the business inside and out. Study your market too. But mostly, you must love dolls!"

◆ ◆ ◆

Nancy Walters: "The first thing a doll artist has to decide is what he or she wants. You can strive for money, fame, artistic reputation, personal satisfaction, or all of these; you probably need to concentrate on one or two objectives, however. Some lucky few manage to achieve all of them in their careers, but most artists are not so fortunate.

"Designing mainstream dolls for commercial production and making molds for the hobby industry are the most likely avenues for reaping financial success. However, there are some one-of-a-kind, fine art-oriented artists who do better financially than some artists who have chosen commercial routes. Unfortunately, hard work and skill alone do not guarantee success; there is an element of luck.

"If you decided, as I have, that artistic personal satisfaction is of primary importance to you, you must do what you enjoy doing and concentrate less on commercially viable work. If you are lucky, the kinds of dolls you want to make will be the ones that plenty of people want to buy. But if you are a little out of step with the masses, selling your work will be harder. I sell everything I make, but I do not have people pounding down my door. I have to look for them in the right places.

"It is also very important for you to develop your own style. While it is impossible not to be influenced by the world around you, your work should not be derivative to the point that people can readily identify the other doll artist(s) who have influenced you. Certainly, they should never confuse your work with that of another artist."

◆ ◆ ◆

Julie Good-Kruger: "You'd better be sure that you really enjoy doing this, because it is a lifestyle, really."

◆ ◆ ◆

Floyd Bell: "Do dolls that you like and have fun with your work. I would advise you to enter all the doll making competitions too. The critiques from judges, shops and other artists that come from this, will be of tremendous benefit and will help you to improve the quality of your work."

◆ ◆ ◆

Ruth Treffeisen: "Well, I believe that a little bit of artistic talent is a necessity. One has to get the hang of sculptural work and creativeness. But the most important thing is the will to work! While creating a new doll, time can not be important. To develop oneself artistically, it is necessary to continuously model and self critique. The development should not be stopped or interrupted by a fast success."

◆ ◆ ◆

Karen Blandford: "Be aware that dollmaking is addictive! Once you start, it's very hard to stop. Remember to always be patient, and if you aren't quite happy with something, put it aside and come back to it later. Listen to the feedback you get from people but never let it discourage you. I sometimes find that the more negative comments spur me on and give me the determination to try harder. When things go wrong, and they will, always remember that these thing happen to everyone when they first start making dolls. You are not alone.

129

"I also feel very strongly that the more work the actual artist does on the doll, the better, as far as the collector is concerned. That's why I do as much personal detailing on each doll as possible. I like my dolls to have all the little hand crafted touches. Many of the costumes call for hand embroidery and I do all that myself. I also crochet the socks for my dolls, even though each sock can take up to two hours to complete. Most of the accessories such as toys and stuffed animals are made by me too. I think that to have someone else paint your faces, sew the costumes or do the little touches would mean that the dolls were less yours. I believe that it is worth the artist's extra effort to ensure that the collector gets the artist's best and most complete work. Dollmaking, like any other artwork, is made to be enjoyed. I make each doll with the thought in mind that it may be the only example of my work that is still around a hundred years from now."

◆ ◆ ◆

**Julia Rueger**: "I think that anyone who even has a glimmer of hope for trying to make dolls should go for it! Read everything you can about sculpting from all different types of artists. Read about colors and fabrics and costuming. Read about the different sculpting materials and how to use them. Then get some clay in your hands and make something! I will tell you the truth though. If you plan to make a living off it right away, you need to rethink your goals, because that's just not likely to happen unless you're a phenomenal artist."

◆ ◆ ◆

**Wendy Lawton**: "I encourage each artist to find their own special niche. I think it's important to develop your own look, your own way of "telling a story." Dollmaking has to be more of a passion than a business, more an idea than a craft."

130

♦ ♦ ♦

Pat Secrist: "The market is very full right now. The toughest time you'll have is getting market identity and shelf space in the store. Do your best work first. When you've got work that everybody around you agrees is your best work, offer it to one of the major companies to produce on a royalty basis. They will handle all of the headaches, produce your doll and make you famous. Then if you want to go into business in a few years, it will be much easier to get shelf space in the shops because people will already know your work. I think that's the best and easiest way to get started."

♦ ♦ ♦

FayZah Spanos: "There are a lot of people who think doll making is as easy as snapping your fingers. It's just not that way. Before you go into any major expense and risk all your savings, be sure that you have a good product to sell. Don't think that just because you've made one doll that it will be a great success. Chances are it won't. Get other opinions of your work. You should also consider the tremendous amount of time it takes to run a successful doll making business. If you're like me, dolls consume your life. There is no time for anything else. I haven't had a vacation with my husband in five years. We have to take separate ones because of the business. If you're serious about making a go of it, you and your family must be really committed to it."

♦ ♦ ♦

Fritz Wolff: "I have a large sign above the door of our conference room in six inch black letters, *'Dare To Dream.'* I think that's an enormously important concept in life. If you want to do something and you dream about it, then go ahead and do it

131

and don't get discouraged or frustrated. None of the world's great artists were born overnight. They developed into what they became.

"When I was teaching sculpting, I saw so many people who would try something and expect to achieve perfection the first time. It just doesn't happen that way but you should still be satisfied and happy with the first one. Just set it aside and start on another one and watch how it gets better. The third and the fourth and the twenty-fifth will be better too. Gradually you'll develop your own special style, but it comes slowly. Give it time to mature."

◆ ◆ ◆

Sherry Stephens: "Before you get into buying a lot of equipment, I suggest you try going to a reproduction dollmaking class and see how you like it first, because making dolls is a lot more work than most people think and it's much more expensive than they expect. If after you make a reproduction doll you still think you want to try and make original dolls, you should start by taking a sculpting course.

"And if you set out thinking to make a lot of money, you might be very disappointed. Most dollmakers start off working for about $1.00 an hour! If you want to make dolls, do it because you love creating and because it's such a wonderful feeling to see how much people like what you create."

◆ ◆ ◆

Rotraut Schrott: "Sculpt your own design, what is in your mind and what you feel you have to do. Do not look to the competitor's dolls to try and work in the same way or copy their designs, but do your own best work from your heart."

132

♦ ♦ ♦

**Peter Coe**: "All dollmakers must be aware that this industry is saturated with mediocrity and extremely low standards of quality. For long-term survival the dollmaker must ensure the highest standard of technical ability and quality of craftsmanship, and this must be a continual process. Successful dollmakers spend years, not months and not just one or two years, but many years honing their technical craft and sculpting skills. Many dollmakers jump from amateur status into exhibiting at major trade shows without doing the "circuit" first. The result has been a gross distortion of the market and at prices that are not sustainable. Remember that there is more to making a full scale doll than just sculpting.

"I would also caution dollmakers to choose their sculpting and dollmaking seminars carefully. Many people teach because they have not made the grade as an artist. Research your teacher's track record in the business."

♦ ♦ ♦

**Janet Ness**: "Don't get discouraged if you don't make a big splash the first year. Be confident in your work. Make sure your work is as good as you say it is, and when you tell a retailer that you're going to be delivering a doll, be sure to deliver it on time. Don't hang them out for months and months. That really irritates them. Know exactly how much you can realistically produce before you commit to it and then deliver what you promised when you promised."

♦ ♦ ♦

**Kathy Barry-Hippensteel**: "I really hate to get my hands dirty. I even hated finger painting in kindergarden, because it was too messy. That's something anyone who is thinking about dolls should consider, and try working with a medium that you can tolerate. I use Super Sculpey because I think it's the least messy. If I go to hell when I die, I think my punishment will probably be sanding greenware and trying to sculpt in Cernit."

♦ ♦ ♦

__Wee Paulson__: "Enjoy your work and don't be afraid to experiment with new ideas. Seminars are great, but I still think trial and error are the best teacher."

♦ ♦ ♦

__Maggie Iacono__: "If you want to turn your dollmaking into a successful doll business, if that's your goal, then you've got to come up with something that's unique, a different approach or a new idea. Then just go with it. Give it all you've got."

♦ ♦ ♦

__Uta Brauser__: "Anyone who thinks they want to become a dollmaker should discover first what they like to create; toys, theater related dolls or puppets, or art objects. And that doesn't include categories for those unique combinations that just happen to evolve out of unconscious "playing around". It is important to focus on a direction, a field to specialize in. Remember, creativity is always welcome in this world!"

♦ ♦ ♦

__Susan Wakeen__: "Winston Churchill gave the best advise I ever heard, at a Yale commencement. When he was introduced to give his speech he stood up, went to the podium, looked out over the graduating class and said, 'Never give up... Never give up... Never give up.' Then he sat down to a thunderous applause. I can't top Winston Churchill, but I would add that anyone who wants to be the very best they can be, should never give up and never stop trying to learn and improve whatever it is they love to do."

Kathy Barry-Hippensteel, 892 Woodlawn Ave., Des Plaines, IL 60016

Floyd Bell, Belle Dolls, 10644 S. Wilton Place, Los Angeles, CA 90047

Karen Blandford, Artist Originals by Karen, 32 Regreme Rd., Picton 2571 N.S.W. Australia

Marilyn Bolden, Mari-Dawn Dolls, 2286 Alligator Creek Rd., Clearwater, FL 34625

Uta Brauser, Uta Brauser Design Inc., 738 Broadway #4B, New York, NY 10003

Paul Crees / Peter Coe, The Paul Crees Collection, 124 Alma Road, Bournemouth BH9 1AL Dorset, England

Julie Good-Kruger, Julie Good-Kruger Dolls, 1842 William Penn Way Suite A Lancaster, PA 17601

*Hildegard Gunze*l, *Studio Hildegard Gunzel,* Dr. Alfred - Herrhausen - Allee 60 D-47228 Duisburg, Germany

Maggie Iacono, European Artist Dolls, 11632 Busy Street, Richmond, VA 23236

Wendy Lawton, The Lawton Doll Company, 548 North First Street, Turlock, CA 95380

Jerri McCloud, Dolls by Jerri, Box 561748, Charlotte, NC 28256

Cindy McClure, Cindy McClure Originals, 13215C S.E. Mill Plain Blvd. Suite 472 Vancouver, WA 98684

Jan McLean, Jan McLean Originals, 255 B Hillside Road South, Dunedin, New Zealand

Janet Ness, J. Ness, Designs, 5808 Irish Pat Murphy Dr., Parker, CO 80134

Betty "Wee" Paulson, Weedidits, 3301 Civic Ctr. Dr. Apt. 18-A, North Las Vegas, NV 89030

Patricia Rose, Patricia Rose Studio, P.O. Box 4070, Anna Marie, FL 34216

Julia Rueger, Julia Rueger LTD, P.O. Box 3282, Crestline, CA 92325

Rotraut Schrott, Spitzingstrasse 85598, Baldham, Germany

Pat Secrist, Apple Valley Doll Works, 1519 S. Badour Rd., Midland, MI 48640-0170

FayZah Spanos, Precious Heirloom Dolls, 807 North Pinellas Ave., Tarpon Springs, FL 34689

Sherry Stephens, Best *Wishes by Sherry Stephens,* 13860-12 Wellington Trace, West Palm Beach, FL 33414

Ruth Treffeisen, Treffeisen U.S.A., 4570 Gail Blvd., Naples, FL 33942

Susan Wakeen, Susan Wakeen Doll Co., 106 Powder Mill Road Box 1007, Canton, CT 06019

Nancy Walters, 690 Trinity Court, Longwood, FL 32750

G.F. "Fritz" Wolff, The Wimbledon Collection, P.O. Box 21948, Lexington, KY 40522

SURVEY

Artists you would like to see featured in future volumes of *Doll Artists at Work*:

_____   _____

_____   _____

Questions you would like answered in future volumes of *Doll Artists at Work*:

_____

_____

Comments: _____

_____

_____

_____

ORDERS

☑ Check all that apply

☐ Please let me know when future volumes of *Doll Artists at Work* become available.

☐ Please send information for quantity discounts of *Doll Artists at Work*.

☐ Please send _____ copies of *Doll Artists at Work* at $9.95 each, plus $1.50 each, for postage and handling, payable to Infodial.

Check enclosed for $_____ (in Florida add 6% sales tax).

Name: _____

Address:_____

City:_____State:_____Zip:_____

Mail to:

INFODIAL
13730 S.R. 84, BOX 211
DAVIE, FL 33325

cut along this line